RECORDING BRITAIN

RECORDING
BRITAIN

VOLUME II

Essex · Suffolk
Cambridgeshire and Huntingdonshire
Northamptonshire and Rutlandshire
Norfolk · Yorkshire

EDITED, WITH NOTES, BY
Arnold Palmer

Geoffrey Cumberlege
OXFORD UNIVERSITY PRESS
in association with
THE PILGRIM TRUST
1947

OXFORD UNIVERSITY PRESS
AMEN HOUSE, E.C. 4
London Edinburgh Glasgow New York
Toronto Melbourne Cape Town Bombay
Calcutta Madras Wellington
GEOFFREY CUMBERLEGE
Publisher to the University

PRINTED IN GREAT BRITAIN

CONTENTS

ESSEX

SUFFOLK

CAMBRIDGESHIRE AND HUNTINGDONSHIRE

NORTHAMPTONSHIRE AND RUTLANDSHIRE

vii

ACKNOWLEDGEMENTS

THE notes accompanying the pictures could not have been compiled without help, and the Editor is glad to have an opportunity to express his thanks—to County Librarians and their staffs; to many members of that accessible and highly knowledgeable body of men, the parish clergy; and to countless local residents who, straightening themselves from weeding or freeing their arms from bags with the week's rations, directed him on his way and imparted odds and ends of information. To the ladies and gentlemen mentioned by name in the text his debt is sufficiently apparent. His grateful recognition is offered, in addition, to Mr. H. V. Anson, Mr. E. A. B. Barnard, Mrs. Monica Dance, Mr. W. H. Eley, Mrs. A. S. Livermore, Mr. David Livingstone-Learmonth, Mr. Percy Millican, Mr. H. D. Molesworth, Miss Lilian Redstone, Miss Georgina Rhodes, Mr. Stuart Syme, and Mr. C. A. Wilson.

ESSEX

Artists

WALTER BAYES, R.W.S.

H. E. DU PLESSIS

FRANK EMANUEL

ALGERNON NEWTON, R.A.

RUSSELL REEVE

W. P. ROBINS

MICHAEL ROTHENSTEIN

KENNETH ROWNTREE, A.R.W.S.

WALTER E. SPRADBERY

ROWLAND SUDDABY

IN 1940 Essex seemed in more urgent need of recording than any other county except Kent. Apart from being an easy target for air-raiders and a convenient dumping-ground for bombs from machines which had failed to reach objectives farther inland, it was also a likely area for invasion, and consequently sure of priority in the attentions of the War Office. Records of Essex, then, were wanted, and quickly, before the county was occupied by the British, or the German, Army.

All this may not have been immediately apparent to everybody. If the trailing lesson of the centuries had been unlearned and the French accepted as friends instead of enemies, the English still thought of the south coast as their front door. By 1940 events were forcing them to look at the map of Europe. They noticed, to their surprise, the northward inclination of the French, Belgian, and Dutch coastline. They found that London was south of Amsterdam. They saw that the lie of land and sea was not the four-square arrangement they had imagined. Things were twisted—even Britain.

Records were desirable for other reasons. Much of the southern fringe of Essex has long been part of Greater London, and this area is not shrinking. But the belief, held by many people living elsewhere, that Essex is suburban in character—what Baedeker describes as a 'dormitory'—has only limited justification. It is a large county, not as flat as it is often made out to be; it has a gentle swell; and as soon as London is left behind, fields and orchards begin to ripple in ever increasing profusion.

The serious historians of Essex are, for the most part, out of date, while the more recent works tend to be, on the whole, not serious, or else to be concerned with nothing later than the Saxon and Roman centuries. Yet few counties show a livelier or more sensible appreciation of tradition. In Colchester, for example, the street names on corner buildings are accompanied by older names in smaller lettering. The museum in the Castle might well serve as a model to most other towns. A periodical, *The Essex Review*, collects historical and topographical information for anyone who cares to use its pages. But pending the completion of the Essex section of the *Victoria County History*, the main authority is Philip Morant; and his book was published in 1768.

EASTBURY HOUSE, BARKING

W. P. Robins

Of this Tudor mansion the Rev. Daniel Lysons (*Environs of London*, vol. i, pt. 2, 1811) observes: 'Eastbury House, an ancient and very spacious brick edifice, stands about a mile west of the town, on the road to Dagenham. . . . There is a tradition relating to this house, either, as some say, that the conspirators who concerted the gunpowder plot held their meetings here, or as others, that it was the residence of Lord Monteagle, when he received the letter which led to the discovery; both, perhaps, equally destitute of foundation.' If, by his concluding comment, the reverend gentleman wished to imply that evidence was weak, he had justification; if he meant that it did not exist, his tone is a little lofty. Though Lord Monteagle was at his house in Hoxton when the anonymous warning reached him, he had also a house at Barking; and the whole story of Guy Fawkes is still so full of holes that even local rumours are worth preserving until they are finally disproved.

In the passage quoted, 'west' of the town is a mistake for 'east'. When, three years later, in 1814, Elizabeth Ogborne published her *History of Essex*, she corrected this obvious slip and seemed to think that, in doing so, she entered the ranks of creative artists; for she lifted the whole paragraph and included it in her text unquoted, unacknowledged, and verbatim.

Recently a museum, now a day nursery, and with an Electricity Depot in brick added to the south-east corner by the Barking Corporation, the house still manages to look, in its walled garden, impressive from any angle. It has lost its eastern hexagonal tower, twin to the one shown in this drawing of the back of the house, but in other respects it has come miraculously through the ages and the war. On the journey there and on the journey away one receives the impression—false, but unescapable—that for miles and miles along the north bank of the estuary Eastbury House is older than anything else by at least three hundred years.

ELM HALL, WANSTEAD

W. P. Robins

A walk down the main streets of Wanstead, three miles from Barking, emphasizes the good fortune of Eastbury House. Two or three reminders of a more inspiring thoroughfare are left, fine houses of the late seventeenth or early eighteenth century; but one is in a sad state of neglect while another, Elm Hall, shows every sign of downright ill-treatment. Even since Mr. Robins drew his picture the scars have multiplied. The lamp and all the windows are now smashed. In the opinion of the adjoining builder, the owner of the property, the place is beyond repair.

The house—it is really two houses in one, the twin half being obscured by the trees—has a noble appearance of brick but, as can be seen, the sides are weatherboarded and so is the back. Examples of weatherboarding have already been given in the Middlesex and Surrey groups, but of all counties Essex was perhaps the most given over to it and contains the best specimens. No doubt the front of Elm Hall was originally wooden. The existing façade may well have been added by some ostentatious vulgarian much deplored in the neighbourhood, and designed by a good architect because the owner could not at that time find a bad one.

SHIRE HALL, CHELMSFORD

H. E. du Plessis

Mid-nineteenth-century topographers commanded a purling, at times a lulling prose; and in this sedative art few, if any, surpassed Thomas Wright. In his room beside the Brompton Road he plied his pen unceasingly for forty years, and thanks to his industry and to his dislike of leaving London to visit the places about which he wrote, by the day of his death there were 129 entries beneath his name in the Library catalogue of the British Museum. Amongst these was his *History of Essex*, which appeared in forty-eight monthly parts between the years 1831 and 1836. It contains the following description of the Shire Hall: 'The Shire Hall is an elegant and commodious building, erected from the designs and under the superintendence of J. Johnson Esq. at the charge of the county; and', Wright ripples on, flowing un-fretted over a tremendous boulder of news, 'being completed at a sum considerably below the original estimate, and to the entire satisfaction of his employers, he was presented with a valuable silver cup, which was voted to him . . . in the year 1792. It is a square building, the front of free-stone, the basement rusticated, with four elegant three-quarter pillars of the Ionic order, supporting a pediment, below which are three emblematical bas-reliefs representing Justice, Wisdom and Mercy.'

The Hall underwent certain reconstruction in 1936, but the façade has suffered little beyond some rather unfortunate glazing of doors and windows at ground-level; and the fine Assembly Room, decorated in the Adam manner, 'with female statues in the Grecian costume', still runs the whole length of the first floor.

Of the fourteen John Johnsons mentioned in the *Dictionary of National Biography*, the one we want was born in Leicester in 1754. He died there in 1814, but most of his working life was passed in Essex, where he was County Surveyor for twenty-six years. His architectural services were much in demand, and another of his works may be seen a little farther down the High Street. This is the sturdy, single-arched bridge crossing the river to Moulsham Street. It bears the date 1787, and when it was built it led the road from Chelmsford through the fields to the quiet hamlet of Moulsham.

QUAY, ST. OSYTH

Rowland Suddaby

Rivers of Essex—the Thames, the Crouch, the Blackwater, the Chelmer, the Colne, the Stour—have a habit of forming estuaries out of all proportion (the Thames excepted) to their size. Deep friths indent the marshy coast, meeting the rivers and creating large islands like Horsey, Mersea, Foulness, Potton, or Havengore, not to mention the numerous small islands and peninsulas. All these creeks are favourite resorts of the hunter of wildfowl and the amateur sailor; they usually contain boats of various shapes, floating or stranded. In a disputed position in the churchyard of All Saints' at Maldon, up another inlet a little to the south of St. Osyth, lie the remains of the Reverend Lawrence Washington, whose sons, John and Lawrence, emigrated to Virginia in 1656 or 1657.

The Colne, which is navigable to Colchester, enters the sea in two arms and provides the village of St. Osyth with two wharves. Here, in addition to the pleasure vessels, there may often be seen boats from the fisheries at Brightlingsea. The tidal mill, on the right of the picture, is of great antiquity and has had some difficulty in avoiding demolition. Like a tottering and decrepit sandwich-man, it is barely capable of holding aloft the board of Mr. Budworth, yacht and boat builder.

THE GREEN, GREAT BENTLEY

Walter Bayes, R.W.S.

One of the finest greens in the country, it is divided by roads into several pieces, any one of which would be a godsend to an ordinary village. Cricket could be, and indeed is, successfully accommodated on two or three of the portions, the annual and celebrated fair for lambs having had, no doubt, through the centuries, a beneficial influence upon the turf.

The green is fringed by the little orchards, gardens, and dwellings of the villagers—weatherboarded shops and cottages, dignified brick buildings of the eighteenth century—and overlooked from the south by the church of St. Mary. Buttercups grow upon it; there is a pond. It is, in short, a noble green, so ample that a resident living opposite the post office or the grocer may be nearly a quarter of a mile from stamps and vinegar.

On every sort of pretext the enclosure of commons continued for at least five centuries, and probably for much longer. 'The movement . . . was halted at last in the decade between 1865 and 1875. It was characteristic of the altered balance of society that enclosure of commons was ultimately stopped by the protest not of the rural peasantry, but of the urban population, who objected to exclusion from its holiday playgrounds and rural breathing spaces. The Commons Preservation Society effectively opposed the destruction of the remaining commons, in the interest, nominally and legally of the vanishing "commoner" of the village, but really of the general public in quest of "air and exercise".' (*English Social History*: G. M. Trevelyan.) The happy scene here displayed thus conceals an adventurous past, and the chances that an artist would depict it in the twentieth century must often have been remote indeed.

THE LIVERMORE TOMBS, BARNSTON

Kenneth Rowntree, A.R.W.S.

No doubt the church at Barnston was dedicated to a saint or saints, but the particulars have been lost; and so, in a sense, its anonymity gives it a peculiar claim to be called the House of God. Here, however, we are concerned not with the church but with the ground beside it.

Country churchyards usually repay examination. At Barnston there stands one of the longest consecutive rows of family gravestones that a connoisseur can hope to meet with. There are nearly twenty in all, and, as many of them mark the resting-place of more than one member of the family, the total of Livermores lying side by side is impressive.

The four stones shown here are near the left end of the row and commemorate four of the daughters of Edward and Sarah Livermore. Martha Susannah died of 'a slow decline' in 1827, at fourteen years of age, and her short life had long been ended, when, thirteen years later, a frightful series of catastrophes struck the family. It was concentrated into sixteen months. In the autumn of 1840 Emma, 'alive and well at noon and dead at night', was thrown from her horse. She was twenty-two. Eight months later Jane, aged nineteen, died of a heart attack, and before 1841 was ended Maria, a London schoolgirl, succumbed to small-pox.

To the visitor a hundred years later, these four stones are more dramatic, or pathetic, than their neighbours; but all share equally, all combine, as evidence of a local continuity to which the modern world looks back with some wistfulness. Close to the sisters lie Mary Ann, the eldest, who lived to be seventy, and their brother, Edward John; then come Edward and Sarah themselves; and, as the line extends, James Isaac, and Sarah Elizabeth, and Charles and Ann, and Charles, and Charles, and William Aaron, and William, and more and more men and women born with, bestowing, acquiring the name of Livermore. There are Livermores in Barnston still.

ST. EDMUND'S, TENDRING

Rowland Suddaby

Where Tendring stands in the north-east corner of the county, not far from the sea, the dying undulations of the land are near their last gasp; and so the church of St. Edmund, being on an eminence (albeit a very modest one) overlooking the Holland brook, is often visible on the level roads round Clacton and Walton-on-the-Naze.

Most of the edifice was built between 1250 and 1350 and thus belongs to the Transition (Early English to Decorated) style; but there have been the usual restorations and more than the usual additions in comparatively recent times. The embattled tower and steeple are only seventy years old, and must be considered highly creditable to the atrocious era which gave them birth. In short, it is a good example of a village church in this part of the world, with walls of stone and flint rubble, often plaster-covered, and a warm-hued, tiled roof. Like most English churches of its age, it has been handed about. For something like four centuries it belonged to the manor, the Old Hall. Then it passed into the possession of the Bowes family, of Brett's Hall. Then it was acquired by Henry Compton, who was Bishop of London from 1675 to 1713. He settled it on Balliol College, Oxford, and there the gift of the living still resides.

THE ABBEY, LITTLE COGGESHALL

Walter Bayes, R.W.S.

Paycockes, a strikingly beautiful house built in the reign of Henry VII, stands on the main street, where it may wrench an ejaculation from the rushing motorist and even, as he vanishes, a glance from his suffused and protruding eye through the back window. The other good, perhaps the still better, thing in Coggeshall has to be sought out. It lies south of the town, past the travelling circuses' pitch, over the river, down a long, gently falling road that leads only to the abbey's scattered remains.

They are, what is left of them, still in use as a dwelling-house and outbuildings surrounded by and enclosing green lawns. They are made of very early brick and flint, and there is hardly one of them that does not contain traces of successive styles, from Norman onwards. To the right of the through-archway seen in the picture a cloister stretches towards the house, and here the superstitious visitor may be startled by a tolerable imitation of the hiss of monks' sandals, provided by a goose, or a gabble of prayers from a guinea-fowl. The usual river slides by, soon to reach, away to the left, a weatherboarded mill overhanging the water. The present mill, though several hundred years old, looks young in the company it keeps, and dresses the part.

Allusions to abbeys have already been made, and there will be many more in the course of the four volumes. The peaceful scene offers an opportunity to note how a minor abbey might be founded, how it could develop, and what was its almost inevitable end. It was a Cistercian abbey, founded in or about the year 1140 by Queen Matilda, who gave the ground and exempted the establishment from taxation. In 1203 King John granted the Abbot leave to enclose a wood, requiring a payment of forty marks in acknowledgement. Under Henry III much more ground was added—on what terms, if any, we do not know. The goodwill of Edward III was secured by the building of a chantrey, wherein a monk prayed daily for the King and his family, in consideration of which the ruler bound himself and his successors to provide a hogshead of red wine once a year. Commercialization was getting into its stride, and from now on there were always ladies and gentlemen anxious to have their souls prayed for, always monks to do the praying, and always farms, mills, estates, and other 'considerations' to be accepted. The abbey which began on a compact site granted by a pious Queen had become a very large landowner indeed when, in 1538, it fell a victim to the Defender of the Faith.

16

BLACK CHAPEL, NORTH END—EXTERIOR

Kenneth Rowntree, A.R.W.S.

The Black Chapel at North End, south of Dunmow, is a 'Peculiar' church—a term of ecclesiastical law applied (in the words of the *Encyclopaedia Britannica*) 'to those ecclesiastical districts, parishes, chapels or churches, once numerous in England, which were outside the jurisdiction of the bishop of the diocese in which they were situated, and were subject to a jurisdiction "peculiar" to themselves. They were introduced originally, in many cases by papal authority, to limit the powers of the bishop in his diocese.'

Practically all these strays were brought into the fold by various Acts of Parliament passed between 1836 and 1850, and it is for that reason that the past tense is employed in the passage quoted above. Nevertheless, there are still, in England, one or two of these churches which managed somehow or other to remain outside the pen; churches where Established services are held uncontrolled by any Established bishop; and the Black Chapel is one of them. It has no resident priest, being managed by Trustees. They choose the preachers, at a fixed fee—though the invitations are now, as a rule, confined to three clergymen who share the ministrations between them.

The ground adjoining has not been consecrated, and so the dead cannot be buried there. The Chapel possesses no licence for marriage, and so the living cannot be wedded there. But the newly born can apparently be christened there at a font which, like everything else about the place, is unusual. It must surely be the smallest stone font in existence.

18

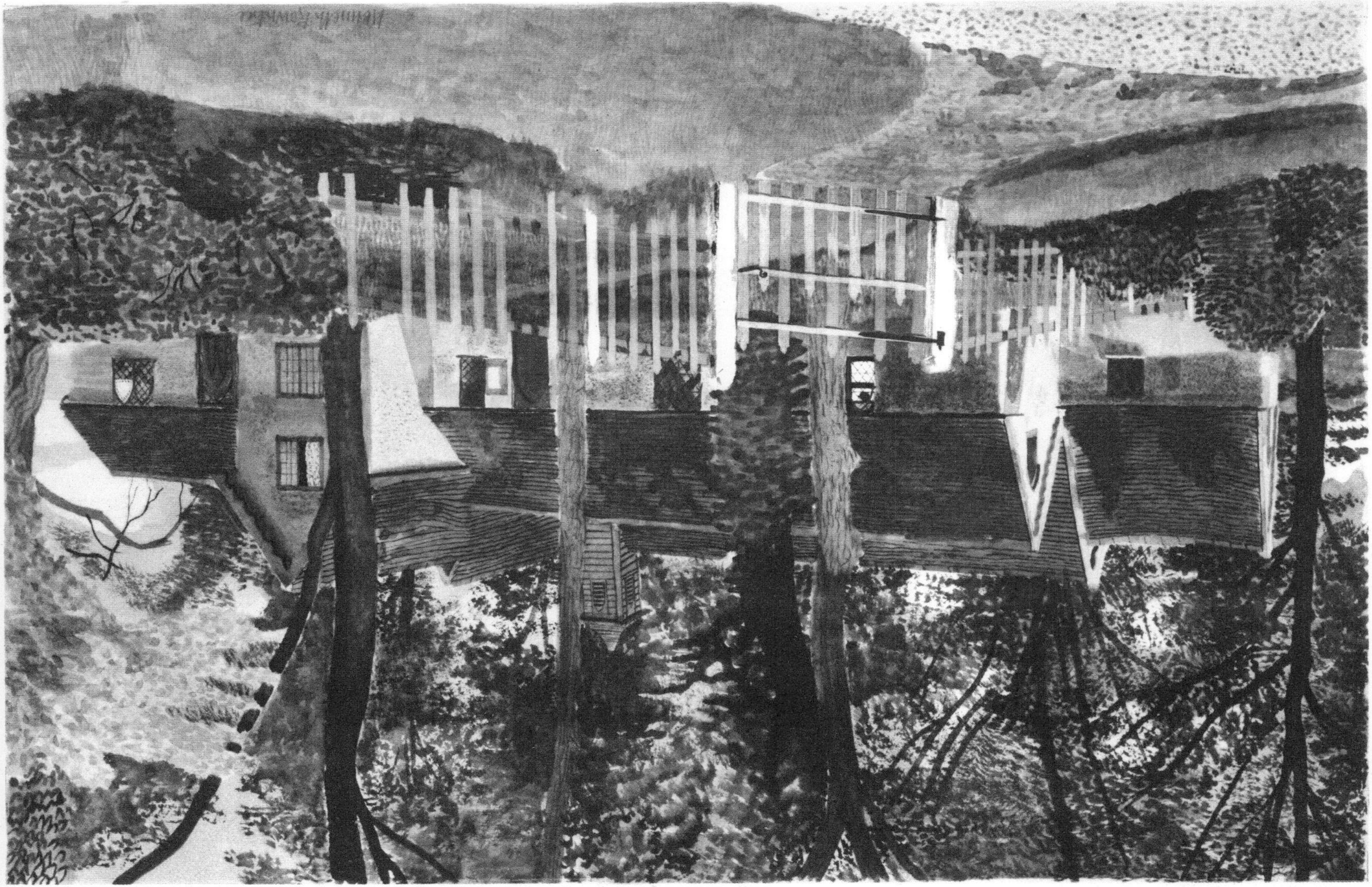

BLACK CHAPEL, NORTH END—INTERIOR

Kenneth Rowntree, A.R.W.S.

The Black Chapel is, indeed, very peculiar. It is as free in its appearance, inside and out, as in its existence. It dates from, approximately, the year 1500, when it was a monastery chapel; but in form it bears so little relation to conventional church architecture, its huddle of roofs reveals such a variety of intentions, purposes, accretions, and afterthoughts that the two drawings serve, far better than any commentary, to suggest the incoherent story.

This view of the chancel shows the older pews (on the left) and the later horse-box pews beneath the double-decker pulpit. Above the screen hangs a framed painting of the Royal Arms, with A. and R. in the top corners and the date of Queen Anne's death (as may be seen) at the bottom. The picture is said to have been carried into the open air on the decease of every subsequent ruler of the realm.

The miniature font has already been mentioned. Over it is a miniature gallery for the musicians. But the many eccentricities of the chapel, so engaging to inspect, must grow tedious in enumeration, and the list may well be ended with the lighting. The position, size, and shape of the windows seem to have been determined less by any notions of pattern or symmetry than by the need to administer from time to time a rebuff, large or small, high or low, here or there, to the denser shadows.

THE HIPPODROME, COLCHESTER

Walter Bayes, R.W.S.

Different people connect Colchester with different things—engineering, founding, Roman remains, rose-growing, boots and clothing, as well as the malting and milling to which allusion has been made. But everyone connects it with oysters. The Romans, who settled here in strength, used to send oysters back to Rome to gladden the drab lives of their families, much as our soldiers, nearly 2,000 years later, smuggled to London the scents and stockings of Rome.

Anyone can easily find for himself the story of the Colchester oyster fisheries. It is enough to say here that they lie at the mouth of the Colne, near Brightlingsea and in other creeks, and are managed by a board consisting of six members of the Colchester Corporation and six members of the Colne Fishery Company. 'The genuine English "native" is produced in its greatest perfection in the Essex fisheries', declares a writer in the *Encyclopaedia Britannica*. With an inscrutable expression which leaves us to guess at his prevailing emotion, he adds that 'it is probably the highest priced oyster in the world'. There was, and no doubt will now be again, a celebrated and annual oyster feast at Colchester; but few people are sufficiently eminent to have been bidden to it, or even to claim acquaintance with those who have.

Colchester is proud of its speciality, and the employment of the shell and pearl *motif* in theatre decoration is merely one manifestation of this pride. Though not an historic building the Hippodrome Cinema is, like many other cinemas, old enough to have begun life as a theatre; indeed, the change from touring companies to touring films seems to have been accomplished with a minimum of desecration, and the words 'Grand Theatre', carved in stone, are still the most solid of the various titles displayed on the façade. Outwardly the building looks contemporary with the station—might well be ascribed to the same drawing-board were it not known that every great railway company retains its own architects and, flushed with their efforts, turns an impatient eye on applicants eager to borrow their services.

MIDDLE MILL, COLCHESTER

Walter Bayes, R.W.S.

Colchester had at one time a great number and variety of mills. It remains a milling centre, but some of the smaller houses have fallen by the way; and Middle Mill is among the casualties. It dates from about 1750, and its inconspicuous career lasted some 175 years. Now, neglected and decayed, it serves as a dump for the Parks and Cemetery Department of the town council.

    With the miller's house adjoining it on one side and the interrupted waters of the Colne making music on the other, it must have been a charming little property. From the mill the view across the pedestrian bridge, in our direction, is still of green meads; on our left, the cricket ground lies spread beneath the castle walls. The rather dressy pinnacle in the distance is something that only the last of the millers can have seen. It belongs to the Town Hall—a building so far superior to its predecessor that when first erected it roused a wave of enthusiasm, now subsiding.

ST. MARY'S, TILTY—EXTERIOR

Kenneth Rowntree, A.R.W.S.

The east end of Tilty Church with its five-light window looks down on the valley of the Chelmer; and there is something startling in its sudden appearance, its loveliness and whiteness.

The village is a small one—about a century ago the population was increasing by one every two years, but this meant twenty in forty years and this, in its turn, represented a rise of 30 per cent—and the church was not built for the villagers. It is part of the remains of a twelfth-century abbey. In some books it is described as the east end of the abbey itself, but more probably it was the chapel to the hospital for strangers at, and outside, the abbey gate. The monks were Cistercians; that is to say, they practised every form of manual labour and neither needed nor admitted helpers from without. But they encouraged a market, especially for the local woollen industry, in a courtyard outside the gate, and they built a chapel there for pilgrims and traders. The present church, or at least the east end of it, was that chapel until the abbey was destroyed in 1535. A similar provision was made at Coggeshall, where there is a corresponding chapel outside the walls.

Mr. Rowntree's drawing displays the principal points of external interest. These, in addition to the east window, are the three-light northern window and the two oddly set niches, partly in buttress and partly in wall. All these occur in the flint end of the church. The western end, where there is a cement surface over brick, was restored by Thomas Maynard in the middle of the eighteenth century. He added the turret, unexpected but elegant. It is practically identical with another church turret some five miles to the south-east, at Barnston, on the other side of Dunmow.

ST. MARY'S, TILTY—INTERIOR

Kenneth Rowntree, A.R.W.S.

Except for microscopic remnants of coloured panes at the west end, all the windows are clear—a feature common enough in the Roundhead counties of East Anglia and, to some people, not a cause of unmixed regret. Bright, pure light is not wanted for the old pews, but it greatly helps the traces of red ochre painting (twelfth-century work) in the architraves, and the notable brasses of the Dannetts and Medeleys. These two intermarried families were of local prominence in the sixteenth century, and their brasses must have been installed very soon after the present church was formed. The other great local family, the Maynards, is represented by its crest— three left hands—let into the stone floor just in front of the altar.

The chancel and the nave were formerly separated, the division being made, perhaps, by the outer wall of the abbey itself, or of the abbey enclosure. There are thus certain duplications, e.g. two sets of piscinae.

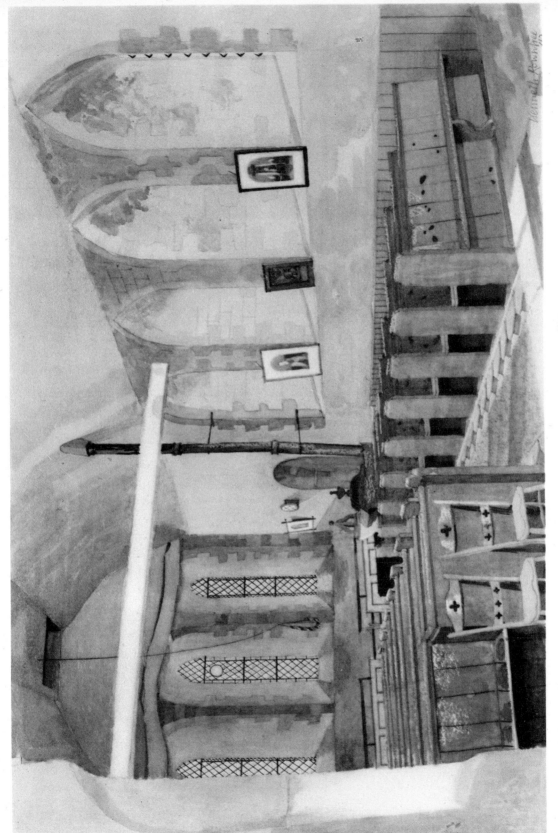

MILL HOUSE, TILTY

Walter E. Spradbery

A field slopes down from the north side of the church. In it are remains of the abbey cloisters, and at the bottom is the mill house. This field, the unillustrated centre of the three pictures of Tilty, is said to have been the first holding in, the foundation of, the estates of the Maynards, who ruled the country-side for 300 years.

The present mill dates from about 1750, and is presumably contemporaneous with the work done by Thomas Maynard on the west end of the church. The original Cistercian mill has been traced a few yards away, under what is now the cowshed; but, of course, the brimming mill-stream, an apparently anonymous tributary of the Chelmer, is a guarantee of continuity of plan.

'An uneven tile roof', writes Mr. Kenneth C. Reid in *The Essex Review*, 'suggested aged rafters and inside heavy oak framing indicated that the brick skin encased parts of the mill standing here at the Dissolution. The ponderous wooden machinery, including a large cog wheel on mountings of the same material, is of course later in date, but it would not differ much in principle from what went before it, because as was the case in the craft of corn grinding, any change which took place prior to the 18th century was small in scale and scope.' The mill is still in use.

WALTER E SPRADBERY

SS. PETER AND PAUL'S, LITTLE SALING—EXTERIOR

Kenneth Rowntree, A.R.W.S.

When the Bishop of Pisa, acting for the Bishop of London, consecrated the church in 1381, it was then a year old. It had taken a long time to build, sixty years; possibly the Black Death, the plague of 1348–9, interrupted the work. The new parish being a sub-parish of Great Bardfield, the vicar of that place drew up a rather tight agreement whereby the parishioners of Little Saling (or Bardfield Saling, or Bardfield juxta Saling) were responsible for part of the cost of upkeep of Great Bardfield Church. In return for that, they might be buried in their own churchyard, but only if they did not fall into arrears with their payments. Owing to an erroneous entry by a clerk they did, in fact, lose control of their church in 1546. In the happy-go-lucky, pre-bureaucratic sixteenth century the mistake was tracked down and corrected within eight years.

The church has a number of irregular and interesting features. (Though the round tower immediately catches the eye, it can be matched by five similar towers in the county.) There is no west window and hardly any east window either, the east end having been apparently truncated and then extended by a low, semicircular addition with a sloping roof. The material of the building is mainly flint rubble, unshaped stones collected from the surrounding fields; but there are a few of the thin bricks known as Roman, and two Tudor bricks near the south porch.

By the road gate on the south side there is a large, round stone, shaped and placed there, in all probability, at least 10,000 years ago. Such stones were set along the recognized tracks, five miles apart, and they marked the spots where Pagan temples stood, and where remains of the Roman and Early Christian churches which succeeded them are apt to be found. The buildings decayed, but the tracks went on serving human feet, the hooves of mules and horses, the wheels of carts; and where they crossed or met there would arise, in time, a smithy, though often enough that smithy, as at Little Saling, is being or has by now been demolished.

SS. PETER AND PAUL'S, LITTLE SALING—INTERIOR

Kenneth Rowntree, A.R.W.S.

The organ in the gallery is a new-comer, purchased in 1933, but it has an honourable history, having belonged to Sir George Elvey (1816–93), the composer of 'Come, ye thankful people, come', 'Crown Him with many crowns', 'Christ the Lord is risen to-day', and other familiar numbers in *Hymns Ancient and Modern*. Elsewhere there are, as in all old churches, plenty of features which invite comment; but in an interior simple to the verge of austerity—unless poverty is a better word—first claim on our attention is made by something even newer than the organ. The cracks on the inside wall of the tower may be compared with the external damage; but neither drawing shows the printed notice in the porch, warning worshippers that they enter at their own risk. One of the last of the secret weapons to fall on England narrowly missed the old building.

When, as already told, the villagers regained possession of their church in the days of Elizabeth, the living was worth some £7 a year. In 1574 a pious parishioner endowed the chaplaincy with a further £3 annually, thus at one stroke raising its value by no less than 43 per cent. One need not be particularly well read to form a notion of the subsequent history of a small living; one goes on getting glimpses. There is, in the third chapter of his *History,* Macaulay's vivid account of the abject position of the country clergy in the time of James II. Everyone remembers Goldsmith's preacher who, less than 100 years later, was considered 'passing rich', and everybody knows Miss Austen's clergymen who, if not very brilliantly placed, if apt to be bullied by their patrons, were incomparably better off than the poor gentlemen described by Macaulay. Forty or fifty years later, Trollope's parsons were again better off and better regarded, the result of Acts of Parliament directed to the more equitable distribution of clerical incomes.

But the insecurity of the clergy was still a source of anxiety when it was suddenly surpassed by that of the churches themselves—a problem beyond the scope of Acts of Parliament, episcopal planning, or the humble congregations of the countryside. Whatever money and material may be found for the gutted but historic temples, for thousands of little churches all over Europe the alternatives seem to be a long tremulousness or collapse.

WETHERSFIELD

H. E. du Plessis

Under at least eleven differing names, from Walperfeld to Wydrysfylde, Wethersfield passed through the usual tremendous adventures of English villages in the long ago. Rarely, it seems, did it enjoy peace until the day when its great landlord, Humphrey Stafford, Duke of Buckingham, Hereford, Essex, and Northampton, fell fighting against his king, Edward IV, at the Battle of Northampton. With much else Wethersfield was then vested in the Crown for a hundred years, when Henry VIII, no doubt to his own advantage, exchanged it with a local landowner, Sir John Wentworth. For a long, ensuing period it remained in the undisturbed possession of that family and had a chance to rest and ripen.

Like Finchingfield, Great Bardfield, and most of these villages, Wethersfield has a green. So great is the variation in size and position that hardly any green can be called a normal one; but Wethersfield's sloping triangle is among the smallest. Temporarily it is not at its best. Engines of war rested on it or used it when, the signpost having been removed at the threat of invasion, errors in direction had to be adjusted at the cross-roads. But with its ten trees—nine limes and a single plane—its wooden seat, and its background of the flint tower and leaden spire of St. Mary Magdalen's, it is a pleasant spot giving, like a well-shaped feature, character and expression to the face of the village.

THAXTED FROM THE FIELDS

H. E. du Plessis

The little valleys of Bedfordshire repeat themselves, like outer ripples, in narrower and shallower undulations in Essex. From the roads in the west of the county there is always a pleasant, never a fine, prospect. It extends from ridge to ridge, the numerous trees displaying no tendency to thicken into woods. Seldom as far as a mile or less than half a mile, the horizon's distance is remarkably regular.

Almost all the views, therefore, are typical, and the landscape reproduced here would hardly be identifiable, even to a native, but for the unmistakable spire. In many parts of England the windmill would be evidence no less conclusive, but not here. On every ridge or every second ridge, windmills are easy enough to find.

The fourteenth-century church is dedicated to St. John the Baptist, Our Lady, and (Thaxted being famous for its cutlery and he being the patron saint of cutlers) St. Lawrence. It calls for a visit on every possible occasion, but hardly for addition to the many existing descriptions of it. In support of the artist, however, it may be said that the spire is no less than 181 feet in height. In the course of its long career it has been struck by lightning and blown down; but for the last 125 years the envious forces have left it alone.

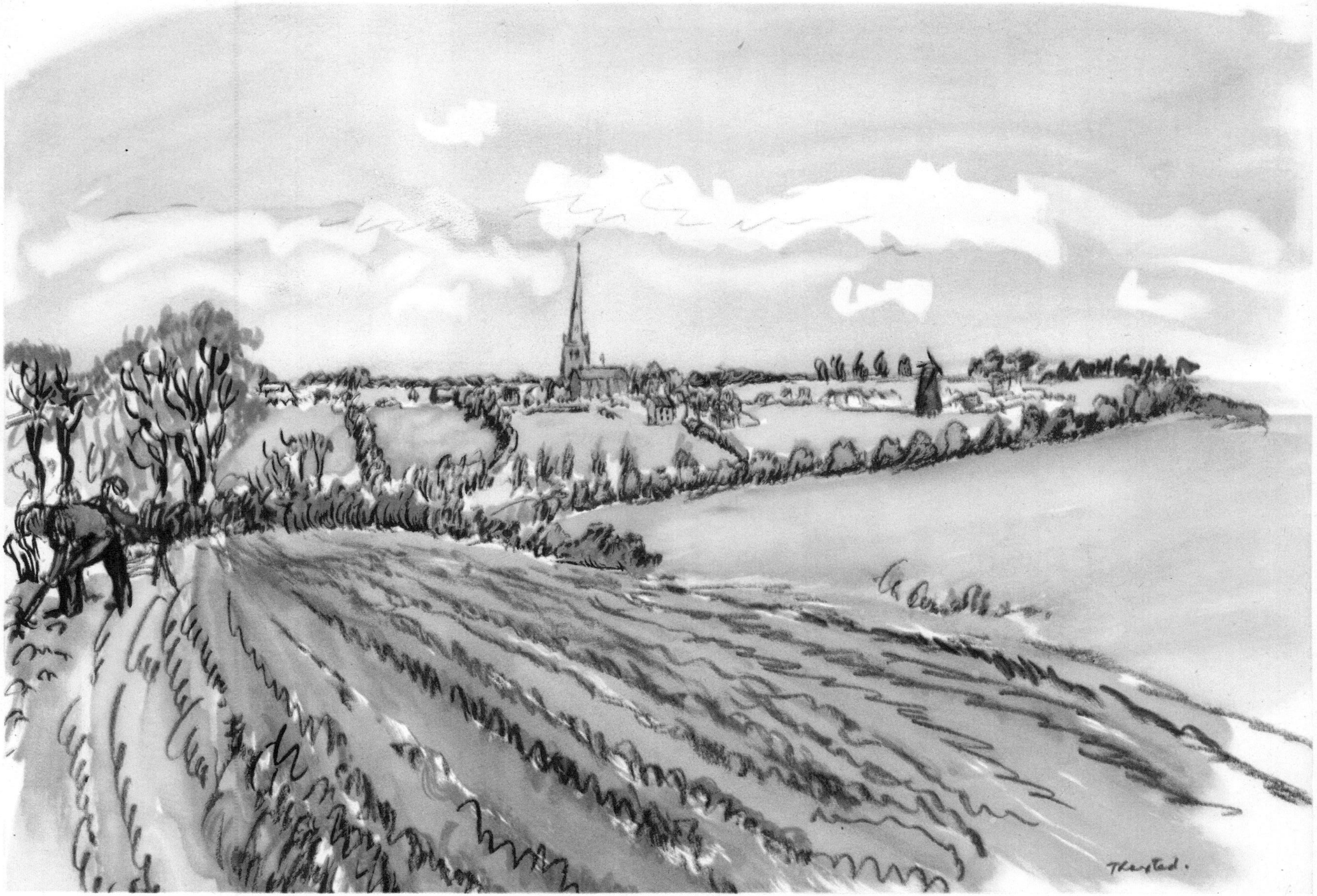
Thaxted.

POST MILL, FINCHINGFIELD

Michael Rothenstein

'This small mill with round-house is very dilapidated indeed. There are the remains of four common sails. The mill has not worked for over sixty years, and it is doubtful if it will stand much longer. . . . It stands on an unusually high mill-hill, largely artificial, something like 20 ft. above the level of the road. It is close to the street, with the miller's house in front of it, and gives a very picturesque appearance over the house tops of one of the most beautiful villages in North Essex.'

The passage quoted comes from the second of two admirable volumes published in 1932 for the Society for the Protection of Ancient Buildings (*English Windmills*: vol. i by M. I. Batten, vol. ii by Donald Smith; Architectural Press). In England, even now, books about windmills are so much rarer than windmills that readers who wish to pursue the matter may find difficulty in satisfying their curiosity. Most of the information contained in this and the succeeding note is derived from one or other of the volumes mentioned.

The post mill at Finchingfield has a circular brick base surmounted by a conical wooden roof. But what, someone may say, is a post mill? Here, in the authoritative words of Mr. Rex Wailes, is a description:

'The post mill is a box-like structure supported at its very middle on the top of a single upright post. Thus it is beautifully balanced so that it may be turned round the post for the sails to face the wind. The post is supported by four sloping struts or quarter-bars, which transfer the weight on it to two cross-trees placed at right angles below the post. The ends of these rest on brick or stone piers. The socket into which the post fits is in the crown-tree, a large beam running the full width of the centre halfway up the body of the mill, much as the top stroke of a T. . . . The mill has to be turned by hand to face the wind by means of a long pole, which sticks out behind. . . . As a rule the mill is so beautifully balanced that it is not very hard work for one man to push it round.'

But sometimes a horse is used.

Some of the features described by Mr. Wailes can be more easily seen in the drawing of the post mill at Fen Stanton in Huntingdonshire.

Michael R. Houston
15 May 1943

GIBRALTAR MILL, GREAT BARDFIELD

Michael Rothenstein

In the sixteenth century a Fleming thought of a better dodge than turning the whole mill; he invented a revolving top or cap. In addition to saving trouble, this allowed the body of the mill to be of brick, resting firmly on the ground, and so at once stronger and less inflammable. The caps were turned either by means of a long pole (the method still used in Holland) or of a wheel with an endless chain or rope. Both methods are practised in England. This new form of stone or brick mill was given the name of tower mill. (There is also a smock mill, which may be briefly and not too inaccurately described as a tower mill built of wood.)

Of Gibraltar Mill, Mr. Donald Smith has the following note (1932):

'If one can imagine an octagon with its corners removed, leaving eight larger and eight smaller faces, one has the external shape of the mill to a height of about 18 feet. The very defective brickwork exposed at the corners indicates clearly that . . . the corners were removed at a date subsequent to the original building. The brickwork at the base is about 4 feet in thickness. At about 18 feet from the ground the brickwork is gathered in and the shape becomes round, and at about 20 feet from the ground the bricks are evidently of a later date than those below. Various theories have been made in explanation of this form. One is that the building is an Elizabethan tower mill that was thrown out of commission . . . but that later it was again fitted as a windmill. Another is that it was built in about 1680 as a smock mill, with a very high brick base. The ascertained facts do not help much to elucidate the problem. They are: that it was used as a cottage in 1749, at which time it was plastered inside and out. In 1751 it was converted into a windmill, and the walls were raised to their present height. The very bold fantail was added in 1904. . . . A further mystery about this mill is the local name, the Gibraltar Mill. By this name it has always been known in local tradition, but for what reason none can tell.'

During the war it was used as a look-out by the Home Guard, who carved a few peepholes, and the sails have suffered further damage by storm since the drawing was made. Their scattered limbs lie on the ground, where at least we can appreciate the astonishing weight and thickness of the timbers.

THE PILLORY, SAFFRON WALDEN CASTLE

W. P. Robins

Down in the dungeon of the Norman castle, now carpeted with grass and wild flowers and ceilinged with the sky, stands a pillory brought from Newport, three or four miles away. As an instrument of punishment the pillory has a long history. This one is not of immense age, but the construction of pillories seems to have reached perfection quickly and few improvements were introduced. The culprit stood on a platform raised some feet above the ground; the top half of the beam was lifted, so that his head and hands could be placed in the holes; the upper frame was then lowered and locked, holding him in an attitude still regarded, even in this joyless age, as tempting. Before being stood in the pillory, a man had his head and beard shaved, a woman had her hair cut off. Large pillories were sometimes made to hold several prisoners, but the single type was the common one.

In the thirteenth century the main offences punishable by the pillory were perjury, forgery, and the use of short weights. Later, thieves (especially of corn or flour), 'bawds and scolds' were added as fit subjects for public execration. Men and women convicted of these unattractive failings must have been considered fair game by the crowd, and their sufferings and indignities may be imagined; but when, in the seventeenth century, the use of the instrument was extended to curtail the free expression of opinion, an appearance in the pillory could become the occasion for a popular ovation. Two unfortunate authors in the time of Charles I—Alexander Leighton and William Prynne—incurred the displeasure of Archbishop Laud, and were pilloried, branded, and mutilated; and seventy years later a far more famous writer, Defoe, was sentenced to be stood three times in the pillory, his offence being a pamphlet called *The Shortest Way with the Dissenters*.

'In 1816 the pillory was abolished except for perjury and subornation, and the perjurer Peter James Bossy was the last to stand in the pillory at the Old Bailey for one hour on the 22nd of June 1830. It was finally abolished in 1837. . . . The pillory was used in the American colonies, and provisions as to its infliction existed in the United States statute books until 1839; it survived in the state of Delaware until 1905.' (*Enc. Brit.*)

The Pillory on the Lower Green, Stepen Walton

BARNS NEAR SAFFRON WALDEN

Frank Emanuel

Little can be said about this drawing; and, as it happens, perhaps nothing need be added to the thoughts evoked in homesick exiles, in cities or abroad, by the simple, indigenous scene.

Buildings of great age abound not only in the neighbourhood of Saffron Walden but in the town itself, where a walk up the main west-to-east street is a history lesson. To the old Tudor houses of the western end succeed in order Stuart, early and late Georgian, early Victorian, late Victorian, and neo-Georgian buildings leading at last to the functional—if that earnest and anxious expression can be applied to a cinema which looks like a schoolgirl delinquent. The paragraphs of the lesson are not quite clear-cut, because people in all ages have been apt to build just outside towns, only to be overtaken by the spread of the next generation. Nevertheless, the story of five hundred years of domestic dwellings unfolds here with unusual precision in a walk of half a mile.

RANKL EMANUEL. SAFFRON WALDEN

SUFFOLK

Artists

JACK L. AIRY	ALGERNON NEWTON, R.A.	A. I. RONALD
S. R. BADMIN, R.W.S.	LOUISA PULLER	KENNETH ROWNTREE, A.R.W.S.
R. T. COWERN, A.R.W.S.	RUSSELL REEVE	ROWLAND SUDDABY
MARTIN HARDIE, C.B.E.	W. P. ROBINS	EDWARD WALKER

OF the first group of artists to be commissioned, eighteen in number, sixteen went to work between Weymouth and Ipswich. Such was the arrangement, eloquent of the state of affairs in the month of April 1940. Before the month was out a batch of four drawings from Suffolk started the collection; on the other hand, three of the artists, unable to begin work immediately, were too late and found their objectives, when they reached them, guarded by sentries and hung with minatory notices. After two years, when the pattern of military control had become clearer and was about to be extended, further recording was done in East Suffolk; but at the time it was thought wiser and kinder to remove the three artists from an area in which, hanging about with their sketch-books and paint-boxes, they were hourly the objects of darker suspicions, and send them to fulfil their commissions in Devon and Glamorgan.

The lot of the artist was not then an altogether enviable one, especially on the east coast. Tact, perseverance, and courage were needed as well as a permit from one Ministry and a guarantee of bona fides from another. One artist, sick of sour looks and grudging concessions, marshalled all the influence that he, his friends, and his friends' friends could bring to bear and obtained a coloured pass of immense power and rarity. In fact, it seems to have been unique, and at the end of a fortnight he was thankful to surrender it and to recover his old and ordinary permit. Never having seen the like of his pink card, the police and military were convinced it was a clumsy forgery from Berlin.

Yet police and military came in time to be regarded by the artists less as a barrier to progress than as a defence against the common enemy, the General Public. The painters were so often reported, and the men in blue and the men in khaki so often roused, that an almost affectionate alliance grew up between them, co-victims of busybodies who, if possibly well-meaning, were fond of results during the lunch hour.

49

BAWDSEY

Russell Reeve

It is fitting that the views of Suffolk, a vulnerable county which is finding some
difficulty in getting rid of its protectors, should begin with the interrupted village
of Bawdsey. It is used to interruptions. Here, during the long months when Boney's
invading forces were expected almost hourly, the Fencibles drilled, and three Mar-
tello Towers were built. Here, in 1918 and the years before, a later generation of
volunteer soldiers fell in, trained, and watched.

The old story was repeated in 1940 and is not yet over. Bawdsey's famous ferry
to Felixstowe is, at the time of writing, still suspended, making necessary the very
thing it was designed to avoid—a twenty-mile detour up and down the estuary of
the Deben for those who would cross the half-mile of water. Two shillings used
to be the fee for a motor-car. A motor-cycle cost sixpence, though an extra three-
pence was incurred if a side-car was attached. No doubt the old service will one
day be restored; but pleasant surprise will be caused if, what with one thing and
another, no reasons can be found for raising the charges.

SUDBURY FROM THE SOUTH-WEST

Rowland Suddaby

Sudbury is no wen, to use Cobbett's word; not a growing and greedy industrial centre, but a country town with an archdeacon. Nevertheless, it has extended, and this view, which must now bear the title given above, would formerly have been labelled 'the parishes or the villages of Ballingdon-cum-Brundon'. Sudbury will in time, no doubt, cross the river Stour and thereby re-enter Essex, to which it was once partly assigned; and it is at that day, near or far, that this water-colour, like so many others here presented, is indirectly aimed.

The Church of All Saints, a building of flint and rubble, dates from 1150, though now mainly Perpendicular in style. There seem to have been two other churches in Ballingdon and Brundon, but this is the sole survivor.

Sudbury is said to have been the original of Eatanswill, of *The Pickwick Papers*. It is certainly Gainsborough's birthplace.

SS. PETER AND PAUL'S, LAVENHAM

Rowland Suddaby

'The church of Lavenham in Suffolk,' observed a commentator in *The Gentleman's Magazine*, 'though now somewhat defaced by the hand of time, still bears the appearance of reverential majesty.' Since these words were written, 160 years ago, the great healer or else the discreet restorer seems to have arrested decay, for the exterior of the celebrated church is now in admirable repair. When, tucked away at the top end of the long curving street, it greets and fills the eye, the most arduous journey is at that instant forgotten.

By contrast, the interior is momentarily disappointing, not so much from the absence of old glass, to which one is accustomed in East Anglian churches, as from the presence of new. But this impression is soon corrected by the roof, screens, chancel stalls, and chapels, as well as by the shape, proportions, and size of the edifice itself. Two fine sixteenth-century chapels with screens of traceried oak commemorate the founders of the church and an alliance between the nobility and trade which, in the fifteenth century, was unusual. The two benefactors were John de Vere, Earl of Oxford, and Thomas Spring, a wool merchant of great wealth.

Like most old churches it possesses, in addition to its beauties, a few curiosities. Perhaps the queerest of these is the inscription on an altar tomb in the churchyard.

> Quod fuit esse, quod est, quod non fuit esse, quod esse,
> Esse quod est, non esse quod est, non est, erit esse.

Such is the decline in classical learning that many a visitor, perusing these lines to-day, can turn away unaffected, unless it be by faint twitchings of a notion to examine once again the works of Gertrude Stein. But in more cultured centuries the verses were the subject of much speculation and translation by scholarly gentlemen. Various renderings, faithful or illuminating, have come down to us. Here is one in which fidelity is the prevailing note.

> What hath been to be, what is it? To be, what hath not been to be what it is to be, what is it?
> What it is to be, what is it? Not to be what is is not, will be to be.

LADY STREET, LAVENHAM

Rowland Suddaby

Lavenham at all times and all turns is capable of taking us back to the fifteenth and sixteenth centuries; but at this corner of the market-place, where Lady Street runs downhill beside the Guildhall, the impression is perhaps even stronger than elsewhere.

The Guildhall, the old timbered building of which one end can be seen in the picture, was set up as a centre for the local cloth merchants—a place of business which doubtless provided also some of the amenities and uses of a club. It is a particularly fine example of village architecture of its day. Door, porch, windows, corner post, and other features all display Tudor England's zest and ability to decorate. Nothing more sharply separates the appearance of our buildings from our ancestors' than the almost total eclipse of that delight and that capacity.

According to Mr. R. H. Mottram's *East Anglia*, a book full of local lore, a blue cloth of its own devising was originally Lavenham's speciality. Under the shadow of standardization, the manufacturers of the town 'later wove in the manner to which the names of Says and Calimanchos, serge and calico, were given'. But Lavenham was too remote to hold its own with the great northern centres, such as Leeds; and that is why, instead of boasting a Town Hall designed by Cuthbert Brodrick in 1853, it can show nothing better than this Guildhall. Its decline, however, was slow. Late in the eighteenth century it was the home of the author of, perhaps, the best-known poem in a literature famed for its poetry. This was Jane Taylor. She wrote 'Twinkle, twinkle, little star'.

WOOL HALL, LAVENHAM

Rowland Suddaby

The Wool Hall, now the Railway Convalescent Home, was the business centre for another thriving local industry. It stands at the end of Lady Street farthest from the Guildhall, yet handy enough for clothiers and wool merchants to discuss prices and materials as often as they wished. Thomas Spring, co-founder of the church, was doubtless a familiar and dominant figure at its proceedings.

So rich is Lavenham in Tudor remains that the visitor, on reaching the building he is looking for, even when that building is the Wool Hall, will often experience a moment of uncertainty in deciding between it, and the house next door, and the house over the way.

MELFORD HALL, LONG MELFORD

S. R. Badmin, R.W.S.

Like Florence and Rome, the neighbouring towns of Lavenham and Long Melford have their jealous champions. There are renowned churches at both, but in most respects the rivals are as different as two places can be. Lavenham is timbered, close, twisting, rambling, Tudor. Long Melford is very long and slender—two miles of early ribbon development—brick built, spacious, aristocratic, Stuart and Georgian.

Such, at least, are the appearances, though the two most important houses of Long Melford are both Elizabethan: Kentwell Hall, on the north side, and the nearer Melford Hall at the east end of the village. Every motorist has remarked this brick house with its four leaden-topped ogee turrets rising above the wall. It was built in 1559, when Mary had been dead a few months only. The first recorded owner, the man for whom in all probability the house was designed, is Sir William Cordell. He had been Speaker of the House under Mary, an office which even at that time, and under that Queen, was reserved, it seems, for a discreet, non-party man. At all events in 1578, two years before his death, Elizabeth visited him at Melford Hall and was sumptuously entertained.

Melford Hall. Suffolk. S.R. Andrew

WOODBRIDGE FROM THE SOUTH

W. P. Robins

Woodbridge was once a flourishing port, closely associated with Yarmouth and a main centre for the distribution and export of butter. Defoe, though not enthusiastic about it, patted it rather absent-mindedly on the head before swishing his rod at the decayed harbours of Orford and Dunwich a little to the north. He compared them unfavourably with the sunken ruins of Carthage, Rome, Jerusalem, Nineveh, and Persepolis; he simply could not understand how their inhabitants tolerated the decline in their fortunes. Not for him the dubious, frequent, penetrating eye with which Shakespeare, a hundred and twenty years earlier, turned and returned to the study of ambition. But we must stick to Woodbridge. In the second half of the last century it, too, began to lose its position in the world of affairs and to settle down, without audible complaint, into a quiet old age beside the broadening waters of the Deben.

Just about the time when Woodbridge was thinking of retiring its decent streets were enlivened by an astonishing figure. Edward Fitzgerald, the translator (if that be the right word) of Omar Khayyám, was born (1809) and buried (1883) some three miles from Woodbridge, and passed almost all his life in houses near or in the town. He was one of those men whose careers do not fit in very comfortably with the social beliefs now prevalent—a slow-maturing man who, but for private means, might never have set and ripened. He liked to take his time; to prune his roses, an art he never mastered; to sail his boat, rather amateurishly; to listen to and talk of music, a subject he understood; and to entertain sympathetic friends such as Carlyle, Tennyson, Thackeray, Charles Keene, and others less renowned. Thackeray was devoted to him. Keene used to sit on his veranda at Little Grange, playing the bagpipes.

But it was not his friends that were astonishing; it was his clothes. 'I can see him now, walking down into Woodbridge, with an old Inverness cape, double-breasted flowered satin waistcoat, slippers on his feet, and a handkerchief, very likely, tied over his head.' That description is lifted from F. H. Groome's memoir. Here is one by another local, though later, hand. 'In these lanes went the tall figure in its tail coat and top hat, plaid shawl, and for bad weather, umbrella, from which his boots would be suspended in warm weather, as he walked barefoot' (*East Anglia*: R. H. Mottram).

TIDAL MILL, WOODBRIDGE

W. P. Robins

First mention of this site beside the estuary of the Deben dates from 1170, when the Canons of Woodbridge Priory granted a plot of land to Baldwin de Ufford, giving easier access to his mill. Later the priory acquired the mill; but neither foundation nor mill flourished and both were in a poor state when Henry VIII 'dissolved' the priory. The King parted with the mill, Elizabeth regained it, and thereafter it had a long succession of owners. Between 1854 and 1874 a man named Alfred Hayward leased, relinquished, and eventually bought the place; and his occupation is notable for coinciding with saturation point in the minds of the neighbours. For three centuries they had been rechristening the mill. As Hayward's mill it is still, and seems likely to go on being, known.

For the following description of the tidal mill and its workings we are indebted to Mr. Rex Wailes:

'The weatherboarding has given place to corrugated iron, but the tiled mansard roof remains. The mill stands on the quay beside the power mill and is served by a pond having an area of 7½ acres with a 6 ft. head. The wooden wheel in a small wheel-house outside the mill was renewed in 1932; it is 20 ft. diam. by 5 ft. 10 ins. wide with closed wooden buckets and is mounted on an oak shaft 22 in. square. A rear vertical penstock is first raised and allows the water to flow over the sluice; the wheel is then breast-shot. The sluice is independently controlled and in two horizontal sections. When the level of the water has sunk sufficiently the top half is raised about twelve inches. Finally the sluice is raised completely and the wheel becomes undershot. It drives four pairs of stones on the first floor, all of which are controlled by a single pair of governors driven from the 22-in. diam. oak upright shaft.'

The post on the left of the drawing has its importance, being the indicator of the height of the tide and of the weight of water.

ST. BARTHOLOMEW'S, ORFORD, FROM THE NORTH-WEST

Louisa Puller

Britain's indented edges have meant strong competition among the coastal towns. Perhaps in no counties more than Norfolk and Suffolk has the struggle been fiercer or the list of casualties longer; and few places have suffered a decline greater than Orford's. At one time this thriving town, standing on a long, curiously shaped inlet formed by the rivers Ore and Alde, had in addition to a castle no less than three churches; the head of the famous Walpole clan took his title from it. To-day it is so shrunken that the castle, which once was in its midst, is now outside its western extremity, whilst its only surviving church, though much smaller than it used to be, is out of all proportion large for a population of 700.

St. Bartholomew's was built a hundred years after the Conquest. Beyond the existing east wall is a Norman chancel which, once used by Austin Friars as a chapel, has been in ruins for over two centuries. But, as has been said, the church is still a large one with a clerestoried nave of five bays. It is notable for its brasses; for the little kneeling figure, in marble, of James I's chaplain, Francis Mason; for three piscinae; and especially for its carved font, with grotesques round the pedestal and, on the western facet, the Almighty grasping the Cross.

Louisa Puller 1942.

ST. BARTHOLOMEW'S, ORFORD, FROM THE SOUTH-WEST

Jack L. Airy

Since artists, compared with cameramen, are slow, it was very seldom that they could be indulged in the luxury of duplication, even though the setting, which means so much to a building, cannot always be conveyed by one aspect. The two drawings of St. Bartholomew's form one of the exceptions to the rule. They show the church from the rural and from the urban sides, in midsummer and in midwinter; and the contrast was thought sufficiently striking.

The ruined chancel beyond the eastern wall has been alluded to. At the western end the tower, or the top of it, is also in a ruinous condition, part of it having fallen down in 1829. On the floor, just inside the south porch, four of the five great bells still stand as they have stood for a hundred years and more, awaiting the reconstruction of the belfry and the restoration of their voices.

ORFORD CASTLE

Martin Hardie, C.B.E.

Date, founder, and purpose of this Norman castle are all unsure. Sir James Mackenzie thinks that, since the ashlar dressings are of Caen stone, it was built in the time
of Henry I or Stephen. The ground was given to Robert Malet (a follower of
William I), and he may have built it. Other authorities have placed it rather later,
suggesting that it was erected by Henry II when at enmity with the Earls of Leicester
and Norfolk. The King's local stronghold, Eye Castle, was inconveniently sited for
the campaign, being cut off from the coast by Framlingham Castle (Bigod, Earl of
Norfolk), and it is supposed that he set up the castle at Orford so as to have access
to the sea and power to check the importation of Flemish mercenaries by his oppo-
nents. All the books tell the story of a merman who was captured in the twelfth
century, brought into the castle, trained, and ultimately set at liberty; but even this
tale has more than one version and is long and disappointingly far from precise.

Only the keep remains, an unusually graceful fragment of castle architecture
seen here from the south. It is a polygon of eighteen sides, with three square and
equidistant towers. The fortress, whatever its size, must have been of considerable
strength. The walls, within which upper galleries run, are solid near the ground
and 20 feet thick; and between the two ditches or moats rose a wall over 13 yards
high.

Through the centuries and down to the present day the castle has changed hands
continuously and frequently, and many names famous in our history occur in the
list of owners. Hubert de Burgh, Philip Marmion, Hugh le Despenser, the de
Valoines, a d'Eresby, a Stanhope, an Earl of Hereford, an Earl of Hertford—all, at
one time or another, have been lords of Orford Castle.

CHURCH FARM, SUDBOURNE

Louisa Puller

Late in 1942 Miss Puller was asked to go, and went at a few hours' notice, to Iken and Sudbourne, villages between the rivers Alde and Ore, where a tract of country was being appropriated for the exercise of tanks and other destructive agencies. Working at top speed she recorded seven farm-houses, some of them with horses, cattle, and poultry rounded up outside the front door and waiting disconsolately for the move. The farm on the opposite page had already been vacated. Like an ageing man caught, for the first time in his life, in the military machine, it is dumb, knowing not what to expect or to do.

A lovely and very large waterside area is still surrounded by barbed wire in red and rusty rolls, and by frequent and rather ill-tempered notices beginning with 'DANGER'. The bordering roads and hedgerows cascade beneath caterpillar wheels, but in the compound itself, where brigades of tanks may lie hidden, there is little to be seen. There, somewhere, stand the deserted villages; somewhere, in there, is Sudbourne Church, which the new vicar has never yet seen; and there are Lodge Farm and Crag Farm, Church Farm, Valley Farm, Chantrey Farm, Hill Farm, and The Firs. What has happened to them all? Are they billets, officers' messes, or powdered rubble? Nobody—nobody living in the district—knows. Partial releases are occasionally promised. Every now and then 'things' appear in 'the papers'. But the most persistent comment, smooth and dark, low and green, high and golden as the seasons revolve, comes from the fields fringing the desolation.

Louisa Puller
1942

ST. NICHOLAS'S, DENSTON

Raymond T. Cowern, A.R.W.S.

A mound in the middle of the village was taken as its site, and there it presides with (thanks to the neglect of the restorers) an air of benign and, some may think, faintly hilarious venerability. The suggestion of rakishness comes from the unusual length of the rain-pipes projecting from the gargoyles' mouths, giving them an expression of irreverent glee rare even in gargoyles.

The clerestoried building is of flint rubble and stone, now much worn, and in the Perpendicular style, with a square, battlemented tower and a fan-vaulted south porch. Within, when at length one passes within, there is not a feature that fails to delight—carved font, east window, pews, roof, screen, stalls, brasses, and memorials. Some of the pews are family boxes, but most are the usual open benches, and all but two of these are of great antiquity, with their oak posts carved into the heads of hares, dogs, and other animals. They gaze up at the roof, where more carved animals, goats, rabbits, and the like, return their age-long stare.

From a tour of the very many beautiful parish churches of Suffolk and Norfolk a man might well come away with St. Nicholas's in the place nearest to his heart. Though of good size, the church is not as large or important as some of the others, but, for that very reason, is better proportioned to the community it serves. It possesses a graveyard that would reconcile anyone to the long sleep. In intrinsic interest and loveliness it can have few, if any, superiors; only in historic associations does it fail, in its class, to reach the foremost rank.

Denston Church - R.T.Cowern

HIGH STREET, NEWMARKET

Raymond T. Cowern, A.R.W.S.

That keen if unskilful rider to hounds, James I, made Newmarket fashionable, and every succeeding sovereign, except George III and Victoria, has been a familiar figure there. In particular Charles II, Anne, and George IV were devoted to it. At the last census the population was below 10,000, and not a little of the town's attraction has always lain in its indifference to going up in the world. The strings of race-horses which pass up and down the High Street early every morning, the news-sheets on sale every evening, are scrutinized more closely than the distinguished visitors.

The square, flag-poled building is the Rutland Arms. Into the yard of the last inn but one occupying this site an eccentric peer, driving from Houghton to New-market in a chaise drawn by four stags, was hunted by the Essex Hounds. The present hotel began as a coaching inn; the bedroom bells hang round the courtyard —little clapper bells on springs attached to a beam on which the old numbers are painted, with 13 already disguised as 12*a*. Down the lane on the left of the hotel a palace, now gone, was built for Charles II under the direction of his Surveyor, Wren; and close by, in Westley's Yard, is the decayed cottage of Nell Gwynne. Besides her came, at one time or another, La Belle Stuart (the original Britannia of our penny), Louise de Kéroualle, Barbara Villiers, the Duchess of Mazarin, and the other ladies. Palace Street is too narrow for manœuvring or myopia, and there must have been some lively encounters. As for the High Street itself, the celebrities who have trodden its pavements would make an endless list. For these pages Vandyck, Rubens, Stubbs, Evelyn, and Pepys may be selected.

The polygonal-fronted house on the left was the Town Hall. It is calamitous that the portico of a building which, until recently, was a peculiarly graceful feature of the main street should be given over to the display of mangles and geysers, with manicure and waving on the upper floor. Before it was the Town Hall it was a cockpit. After a forenoon's hawking Charles II (far from being the effete creature of vulgar belief) would spend the afternoon riding races (he went to scale at 13 st.) or at cockfighting, and the evening gambling, dancing, or at the play. He would have thought little of the bucks of the Regency, with their 'billiard and other rooms for . . . those gentlemen who prefer games of skill, or hazard, to the more boisterous Diversions of the Turf'.

Newmarket . High Street .

R.T. Cowern - 1940

HIGH STREET, NEWMARKET, ON A TUESDAY

Raymond T. Cowern, A.R.W.S.

Here is the same street a few yards farther west, with the Rutland Arms just out of sight on the left, on the other side of the road, in Cambridgeshire. The pavement and houses on the right are in Suffolk, to which county Newmarket is assigned.

In 1227 Henry III granted the right to hold a market in the town every Tuesday. Horses came into the deal even then; the King received two palfreys in return for his favour. Tuesday is still market-day. It would be pleasant to describe buxom dairymaids selling butter and cheese and village craftsmen offering chairs, tables, and bowls designed and shaped at home. But though some local produce, like vegetables, fruit, and flowers, is to be seen, most of the stalls are laid with cheap stockings, ornaments, and cosmetics, and served by swarthy orientals from the east end of London. These traders bring their goods by car, and not only at Newmarket, a 70-mile run, but at towns much farther from the metropolis these same men and women, or their doubles, appear every week on market-day. The expenses of transport and the rent (ten shillings or so) of a stall evidently amount to much less than the profit to be made by each of several competitors selling identical articles. From the ratepaying shopkeepers across the pavement far better value is usually obtainable; but through the centuries the attraction of the pedlar has grown deep roots, especially the pedlar from distant lands. It is very possible that a man in a tarboosh, with mats over his shoulder, was found smiling, on a good pitch, on that original Tuesday in 1227.

This drawing was made not long before a day-raider, roaring over the town, dropped a stick of bombs down the right side of the street. But the High Street, though practically every house is now a shop, retains its engaging air. The factors are good—broad roadway, spacious pavements, harmonious buildings designed, at varying periods, for comfortable domesticity or elegant relaxation—and it is to them, and to the avuncular authority of the Jockey Club, that the old town perhaps owes its powers of resistance and assimilation. Annually, between April and November, it is swamped by visitors on thirty days, and again in December, but such is its vitality that it influences its crowds more than they influence it. To its history and character Baedeker was strangely insensitive; he mentions it with the pursed lips familiar in his references to certain places of entertainment on the Continent; and one is led to wonder if he lost money there or, through over-caution, ignored advice by which he might have covered his expenses, and more.

78

"Market Day - Nunmarket - R.T. Conrad. 1940

MARKET STREET, NEWMARKET

Raymond T. Cowern, A.R.W.S.

When Newmarket first became fashionable, in the seventeenth century, it was a very small place, not nearly big enough to accommodate even the Court. Officials as eminent as the Lord Chamberlain had to sleep under canvas.

In two or perhaps three streets, of which Market Street is one, can be seen the little houses in which the nobility and ladies were glad to lodge, doubtless competing to book rooms for the whole season in the same way as regular racegoers do to-day. These warped roofs, bow windows, and weatherboarded fronts have shielded wild parties, for it was the custom to end a day on the heath with a night of heavy gambling. It is pleasant to be able to state that they have not descended to the dealers in bogus antiquities or peasant ware, but are occupied by a chiropodist, a *coiffeur de dames*, and similar vital practitioners.

When this drawing was made the old by-way was intact. The far right-hand corner—out of sight here—where Market Street runs into the High Street was soon afterwards demolished by the day raider. At the near end, to right, to left, and behind us, the street breaks up into quiet courts and passages; and if, as may happen to anyone in Newmarket, you particularly want to see a man, to whisper out of the corner of your mouth or to bend an ear, Market Street is as safe a place as any.

Newmarket.   R. T. Cowen. 1914.

DALHAM

Raymond T. Cowern, A.R.W.S.

Dalham, five miles east of Newmarket, only just escapes having, as its sole marginal note, 'a fine avenue of beech-trees'. But there was an hour, not so long ago, when it seemed about to become a household word throughout the Empire. The air of this leafy village suited Cecil Rhodes: he found that at Dalham his labouring heart could support the task of breathing more easily than elsewhere, and he bought the old house built, in 1704, by Simon Patrick, Bishop of Ely. The big plane-tree outside the mansion is the slightly smaller relative of the one in the Palace grounds at Ely.

When—the personal privations and wranglings in besieged Kimberley, added to his wider anxieties for the fate of his life's work, having finally broken his health—Rhodes returned to England, he passed one day at his newly acquired property, the only day, it is said, he ever spent there. He died at Muizenberg three months later, at the age of 49, leaving the estate to his nearest relatives. 'I object', ran a testamentary instruction of the great but unmarried proconsul, 'to an expectant heir developing into a loafer.' Before thirty years had gone by, Dalham Hall was owned by a different family with a different name.

Oakham —   R. T. Cowern — 1940

BARTON MILLS

Raymond T. Cowern, A.R.W.S.

On leaving Newmarket the main London–Norwich road runs beside the Limekilns gallops and Waterhall Farm, crosses the railway, passes through the pine trees which mark the sandy tongue thrust south from Worlington, and comes to the old coaching inn, *The Bull*, at Barton Mills. Here it turns sharply to the left, feels its way, rather blind and shrunken, for a few hundred yards, when it reaches a major signpost which waves it away in four level, wide-open directions, to Littleport, to Brandon, to Thetford, to Bury.

The mill beside the bridge over the river Lark stands in the obstinately old-fashioned stretch leading to the junction. By an extraordinary, but not uncommon, distortion of language, this gentle scene has been condemned as dangerous and lies under capital sentence. In the age of the internal combustion engine, dangerous is the bully's word for inconvenient; and the real crime of this particular piece of thoroughfare consists in imposing an 'unnecessary' touch on the brakes some seconds before it becomes necessary at the crossroads.

The drawing was made in June 1940, at a time when everybody knew that German parachutists would be dropped, though nobody knew where. In the course of his work, the artist became conscious of the presence of a Local Defence Volunteer with a levelled rifle in his hands and pumps on his feet. A colleague who joined him was dispatched for the police, and returned with two of them. They examined Mr. Cowern's passes and permits, folded them to the official size of the official note-book, and were only with great difficulty restrained from treating the drawing in the same way. Finally, after being marched to the police station at Mildenhall, a mile and a half away, and listening to the sergeant's decided views on the conduct of all concerned, Mr. Cowern found himself free to resume the task interrupted two and a half hours earlier.

Barton Mills - R. T. Conan - 1940.

FRAMLINGHAM CASTLE, FROM THE NORTH

Martin Hardie, C.B.E.

No better chance will occur to illustrate the part once played by the castles whose ruins may be seen in every county. The note below summarizes, in five minutes, a very considerable lesson in English history. For a fuller account see *The Castles of England*, by Sir James D. Mackenzie.

A Saxon stronghold stood here in which Edward, King of the East Angles, was besieged in 870 by the Danes. Little more is heard of it until, in 1103, Henry I granted it to Roger Bigod. Roger's son William was drowned with Prince William in *The White Ship* at Barfleur in 1120, and the property passed to his brother Hugh who, after swearing allegiance to Henry II, threw in his lot with Henry's rebellious sons. He seems to have attracted the King's especial wrath and was hunted from castle to castle. In 1175 Framlingham was demolished and its three moats filled. Hugh, however, escaped and managed to secure pardon; by the time he died, crusading, two years later, he was Earl of Norfolk. His son Roger, one of the leading agents of Runnymede, must have rebuilt the castle, for John captured it in the year of Magna Charta. John died twelve months later, the Bigods recovered Framlingham and held it until, heirs failing, it was bestowed by Edward I on his fifth son, Thomas of Brotherton. By female branches it descended to the ancient and noble house of Mowbray, Dukes of Norfolk and hereditary Earls Marshal of England, where it remained till the sixteenth century, when (the family name being now Howard, not Mowbray) sundry executions and threats of execution by Henry VIII took effect.

Edward VI granted the castle to his half-sister, Mary. At his death she left her estate at Hunsdon and started, as some say, for Kenninghall, her Norfolk seat, or, as seems more likely, for London; but, learning that Lady Jane Grey had been proclaimed Queen by the Privy Council, she hesitated, and then rode hard for Framlingham—a good place for defence and, if things went ill, handy for Aldeburgh and a ship to Flanders. She immediately flew her standard from the gatehouse, and 13,000 gentlemen and peasants of Suffolk, as well as ships and volunteers from all parts, put themselves at her service. A month later she entered London. She restored the castle to the Howards (to this day the chief Catholic family of England); but nineteen years later, in 1572, Elizabeth found that the 4th Duke of Norfolk was in communication with Mary, Queen of Scots, had him beheaded, and seized his property. James I for the last time restored Framlingham to the Howards. In 1635 they sold it to Sir Robert Hitcham. In 1639 it was dismantled and passed into a ruin.

ST. PETER'S, THEBERTON

Jack L. Airy

The roof is thatched. According to Hugh Bryant's careful records of the county parishes, eighteen churches with thatched, or partly thatched, roofs still, in 1912, survived the improving zeal of the nineteenth century. Lest it be thought that the twentieth century has lagged, the reader can be assured that there are not eighteen now; but, besides Theberton's, examples can be seen at other places like Uggleshall and Fritton.

Norfolk and Suffolk being destitute of building stone, thatching was an easy, effective, and cheap way of roofing as long as thatchers were plentiful. That race is now dying, but all round Theberton noble thatchings meet the eye and cheer the heart and prove that the secrets of the profession are not yet forgotten.

St. Peter's, a mixture of Norman and Perpendicular, is principally of the fifteenth century. The south chapel is full of murals, windows, and other memorials of Doughtys, the family at the big house, The Hall, where on 19 August 1843 Charles Montagu Doughty was born. One likes to hope that the author of *Arabia Deserta* will be remembered longer than Count Zeppelin, and that even an air-minded posterity will be drawn to the south chapel rather than to the grave, in the church-yard, of sixteen Germans, members of the crew of *L 48*, destroyed over Theberton in the night of 17 June 1917.

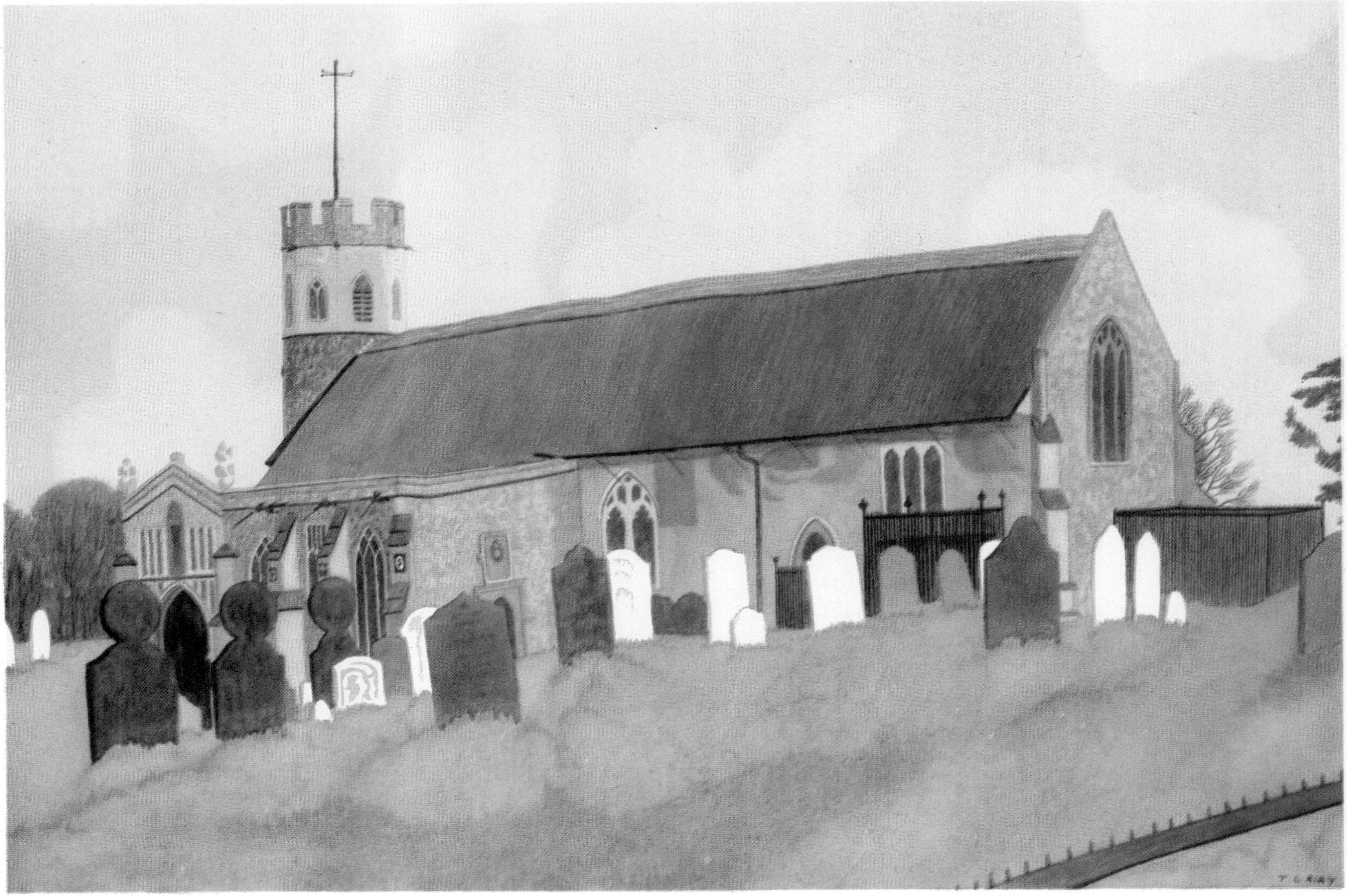

CAMBRIDGESHIRE AND HUNTINGDONSHIRE

Artists

GRACE GOLDEN   BARBARA JONES

P. TENNYSON GREEN   EDWARD WALKER

MARTIN HARDIE, C.B.E.

BOTH counties invite external comparisons. Cambridgeshire, like Berkshire, is long and sprawling; its southern border marches with the almost metropolitan Hertfordshire, while at the other end it merges into far-away Lincolnshire. It is nearly sixty miles in length, yet it possesses only one important centre, and that a University city. Its large rural areas—not dictated to, not dragooned, not exploited —have retained such varying characteristics as are apt to be found in so long a span. The recording of Cambridgeshire on a limited scale was thus not easy. It demanded more artists and more time than could be afforded and, to be brief, it was destined from the first to be left in a suspended and introductory condition. The villages in particular call for endless recording, and since communications, never very good, were in war-time often less than adequate, they had to remain virtually untouched. The task is well worth doing; there is time for it to be performed with care and devotion; and good homes, from the beautiful Fitzwilliam Museum downwards, await the results.

The small county of Huntingdonshire, like the still smaller Rutland, is also free of manufacturing centres, and its largest town has a population of four thousand. Except for the rushing menace of the Great North Road it is compact of peace. From its quiet fields, none the less, there burst forth, three hundred years ago, the principal disturber of our history, Oliver Cromwell; and, for the casual visitor, he yet haunts the scene.

Although one-seventh of the county is included in what is known as the Fen District, Huntingdonshire has hardly room enough to change its character, to play more than one part. Almost any place is a mere bicycle ride from another; almost everything is pleasing, well set, and typical of the rest. In spite of the many beauties, not many drawings were made here since they hardly seemed to be needed. The county can be recorded with ease and something like thoroughness whenever a benefactor so decrees.

KING'S PARADE, CAMBRIDGE

P. Tennyson Green

Very little danger to this famous prospect is likely to come from neglect, but from change masquerading as improvement nothing is safe. The small houses on the left will not last for ever, have not all lasted; and replacements usually consist of something a little, or a lot, taller. There are signs of the horrid tendency here; they are still more marked in the succeeding picture.

King's Parade is very short and very distinguished. It begins at the Senate House (a corner of which appears in the right foreground), built in 1722–30 by James Gibbs, architect of St. Martin's-in-the-Fields and St. Mary-le-Strand in London and the Radcliffe Camera at Oxford. Obscured by it is the old University Library, now the Law Schools, and the next visible landmark is the roadside screen to King's College, its crocketed pinnacles echoing the chapel's. This screen was erected in 1824–8 to the design of William Wilkins, architect of the National Gallery and University College, London, as well as of much else in Cambridge. And there King's Parade ends, and the road takes and for some way southwards keeps the name of Trumpington Street. As such it passes the Bull Hotel and the colleges of St. Catharine's and Peterhouse where, amid formidable gutters and memories of old Hobson, it disappears from this picture. The square, ecclesiastical tower rising in the background belongs to the Cambridge University Press, and for obvious reasons is sometimes known as 'the Freshmen's church'. The building, the original building, had a queer history. A committee for erecting a statue to Mr. Pitt, in London, collected far too much money for its purpose, and in 1824 the surplus was offered to, and accepted by, the University Press and expended on new premises.

In the left foreground, framing the drawing, can be seen the extreme west end of Great St. Mary's, the University church. St. Mary's Passage, just beyond, leads to Market Hill and the next page.

MARKET HILL, CAMBRIDGE

Grace Golden

With King's Parade, from which it is separated by the university church, Market Hill forms the heart of Cambridge. It is a large square, the centre of which is filled with stalls and parked cars, and the visitor usually, naturally, and truthfully refers to it as the market-place.

Some stalls are occupied every day, and all stalls on some days, and it is perhaps owing to this arrangement that Cambridge has retained a fairly firm hold on its market—firmer than the larger Norwich, for instance, or the smaller Newmarket. University towns must be well provided with bookshops, and one or two second-hand dealers may always be found offering attractive selections, doing brisk business, and taking up a good deal of room in the process. Books, fruit, flowers, and vegetables do not leave much space for the London invasion.

The abominable tendency of buildings to grow higher is already spoiling the proportions of the square; nor are there many remaining details which catch and hold the eye. On the east side is a tile-hung house, now the office of a tourist agency, where the old shell canopy surprisingly finds itself preserved above the first-floor window.

Grace Golden.

ST. MARY-THE-LESS, CAMBRIDGE

P. Tennyson Green

Peterhouse, the oldest college in Cambridge, was founded in 1284, and took its name from the church of St. Peter which stood beside it. The church served as the college chapel until, in spite of the reputation of its patron saint, it fell down just over half a century later. A new church was built on the site and dedicated, 3 November 1352, to the Blessed Virgin Mary. When the University church, though of subsequent date, was also consecrated to St. Mary, Peterhouse chapel became known as Little St. Mary's, or St. Mary-the-Less. It served the college for 350 years, until a separate chapel was erected.

The features of the interior belong, as usual, to different periods. The best known are the east window, noted for its tracery, and the mural tablet to the memory of Godfrey Washington, of Yorkshire, who was vicar from 1705 to 1729. The embryo stars and stripes of the Washington arms break the pediment of the tablet, and the reverend gentleman has been commonly, though not finally, accepted as the great-uncle of the first President.

Previously, in 1639, Richard Crashaw, the mystic poet, had been vicar, or something like it; he held the Roman faith, and the position is obscure and irregular. But since, by one of the ironies of sightseeing, the personal and anecdotal have a pull over all other considerations, it is for the sake of another poet that most visitors wander round to the south side of the church, where a window of the adjacent college buildings is crossed by an iron bar. Thomas Gray, who had been an undergraduate at Peterhouse, returned and lived there for some years, writing many of his finest poems behind that window. He had a dread of fire—well founded in those days of port-sodden men staggering with candles up wooden staircases to panelled rooms—and in January 1756 he ended a letter to his friend Wharton with these words: 'I beg you to bespeak me a Rope-Ladder (for my Neighbours every day make a great progress in drunkenness, wch gives me reason to look about me) it must be full 36 foot long, or a little more. . . .' The fixing of the bar and the arrival of the ladder did not pass unnoticed by the undergraduates. In the middle of a February night there was an alarm of fire; the new ladder worked beautifully; and Gray descended from his window into a tub of water placed ready to receive him. The sweetest natured and most lovable of men failed to appreciate the joke and moved within a few days across the road to Pembroke, an address he kept till he died.

CHAPEL OF ST. MARY MAGDALENE, STURBRIDGE

P. Tennyson Green

Like St. James's Palace in London, Sturbridge was originally a hospital for lepers. When, after serving in this way for 500 years, the London site was annexed by Henry VIII for the erection of a new residence, he granted the hospital an alternative position in Suffolk. When the Sturbridge hospital was demolished in the same reign, the chapel was spared, but no other provision for the patients seems to have been made.

Nothing is known of its foundation. It is first mentioned in 1199, but the chapel (and presumably the hospital to which it belonged) is judged to have been by then in existence for some seventy-five years already. No remains of the hospital, the master's house, or any other building have been found. The ground, on the east side of Cambridge, was doubtless chosen for its isolation; and when, in 1272, the burgesses complained that the Warden was no longer maintaining lepers as he was bound to do, they were presumably annoyed less by his enjoyment of a sinecure than by his failure to remove deadly infection from their midst. They may also have had an eye on the Fair tolls which, granted to the Wardens by King John, were eliciting no service in return. These tolls must have been considerable. The Sturbridge Fair (it is still held) was the biggest thing of the kind in Europe until surpassed by Nijni Novgorod in the eighteenth century.

The chapel, some 50 feet long by $12\frac{1}{2}$ feet wide, is strongly built of flint except at the lower (chancel) end, where the walls are faced with ashlar or square-hewn stone. In 1816 the Rev. Thomas Kerrick bought the chapel for £160, presented it to the University, and opened a subscription list for its repair. Further repairs or restorations were effected in 1867 by Gilbert Scott, who was at that time engaged on the erection of the chapel at St. John's College. In spite of its evident points of interest and beauty, the little building was, a few years ago, exhaling a dank, forsaken air. But it has now been warmed back to life by services held there every Sunday in term-time by the students of Westcott House, a Training School for Clergy.

CLOCK TOWER, FEN STANTON

Edward Walker

On its way from Cambridge to Godmanchester and Huntingdon the Roman *Via Devana* becomes, for a few minutes, the High Street of Fen Stanton. It regains its liberty at the Hilton crossroads, and at this point stands the Clock Tower, looking eastward through the village.

It is a square building of brick made redder still by the application of a paint or distemper of dramatic hue. The bell in the round-arched, timber cupola was cast by Thomas Norris in 1660 or 1666, and the structure itself is of approximately the same date. It was intended to serve, and served, as the lock-up or police cell. Now it shelters beneath its extended front the self-incarcerated patrons of the bus service. The old clock goes well, its handsome face is kept fresh and clean, so that almost everyone in Fen Stanton need only look out of the window to tell the time.

POST MILL, FEN STANTON

Edward Walker

This drawing and note will be more intelligible if taken as supplementary to pp. 40–1, where will be found a picture and an explanation of a post mill in comparatively recognizable shape. Here again at Fen Stanton is the circular brick base to protect the base timbers and to provide extra storage-room. (This one is now a hen-house.) Here one may see what Mr. Wailes meant when he described a post-mill as 'a box-like structure'; the single upright post, 2 feet in diameter and rounded where visible, though square beneath the roof; the crown-tree running across the body of the mill at a point half-way up.

The following details (taken from a paper appearing over the name of Mr. C. F. Tebbutt in the *Transactions of the Cambridgeshire and Huntingdonshire Archaeological Society*) may help to tidy up a few queries in the reader's mind. All post mills now remaining are probably of the eighteenth century. The cogs were usually of horn-beam or apple, easily renewable; the central post and the box were always of oak; the sails of pitch pine. The mill shown here is the last of four mills that stood on the road from St. Ives to Fen Stanton. The round-house beneath the conical wooden roof is built of 2-inch bricks, and so are the interior supports for the cross-trees to which, by means of four sloping struts, the weight on the post is transferred.

Near Fen Stanton
Huntingdonshire
Edward Walker
June 1941

THE MILL, HOUGHTON

Martin Hardie, C.B.E.

Praise of the beauty of this seventeenth-century mill or of its setting is made unnecessary by Mr. Hardie's picture, wherein is neither flattery nor omission.

The village of Houghton, midway between St. Ives and Huntingdon, is a small one; yet the mill, little more than a hundred yards from the centre, has to be inquired for and sought out in its secluded position. It is one of a long line of mills standing here beside the Huntingdonshire Ouse, the first—or the first to be mentioned—having been presented by Earl Ailwin to Ramsey Abbey at its foundation in 969. The existing house is three-storied, with attics above, and the timber frame is boarded over. During the nineteenth century the property was owned by Messrs. Potto Brown and Joseph Goodman, millers and philanthropists of note, and it continued to be worked by their descendants until well into the present century. Now it is used by the Youth Hostels Association, a happy arrangement which keeps the old place occupied and provides selected holiday-makers with long and innocent hours spent in flogging the stream. According to the rules of this attractive organization, youth begins at nine and then stays for good.

ELY FROM THE SOUTH-EAST

Martin Hardie, C.B.E.

Readers unfamiliar with the eastern counties of England may be struck by the recurrence, in the notes on the churches and castles, of such phrases as 'standing on a mound' or 'perched on a small eminence' or 'overlooking the village'. Important buildings in this quarter of the kingdom are usually on slight rises; it is almost true to say, in reverse, that slight rises are usually occupied by important buildings.

This was not brought about solely by considerations of dignity or defence. Dry vaults and solid foundations had yet stronger claims. In and around the Fen District, where waterlogged or flooded fields were once an accepted feature of the landscape and men for centuries lived amphibious lives, there were seasons when the higher areas stood up like islands amid the surrounding wastes of water. Something of the same effect, some idea of conditions in the past, can still be given by prolonged spells of wet weather.

The old term 'Isle of Ely' covers the northern end of Cambridgeshire, but the aspect of Ely, no matter how often it is seen, never fails to lend it a more limited significance. The cathedral, raised a few yards above the fens, is visible for miles; and many a traveller confused by the endless, geometrical repetitions of the canals has blessed the white gleam of its roof. Again, Defoe noted that 'as these Fenns appear cover'd with Water, so I observ'd too, that they generally at this latter part of the Year appear also cover'd with Foggs, so that . . . the Isle of *Ely* look'd as if wrapp'd up in Blankets, and nothing to be seen, but now and then, the Lanthorn or Cupola of *Ely Minster*'. The picture, one of a group of watercolours presented by the artist to mark his sympathy with the Scheme, was painted from the Soham side.

NORTHAMPTONSHIRE AND RUTLANDSHIRE

Artists

S. R. BADMIN, R.W.S.	JOHN PIPER
BARBARA JONES	MICHAEL ROTHENSTEIN

JULIAN LEATHART

NO such urgency, no such adventures as marked the recording of the counties on the North Sea, stressed the work in these two shires. In addition to its inland position, Northamptonshire disclosed another reason for deferment. It seems to be, on the historical and topographical side, one of the best-organized counties in the kingdom; a highly distinguished and influential committee looks after its local and traditional amenities; detailed information was not merely forthcoming, it was ready and waiting; and, in brief, Northamptonshire showed itself, of all the counties where our artists journeyed, the most capable of managing its own recording, though far from being the least glad to see it done.

Rutland, too, lacked urgency, though for different reasons. Northamptonshire has its industrial centres; it 'may be said to stand chiefly on other men's legs' by providing them with boots and shoes. But our smallest county seems at present to face no danger of any kind. It has no manufactures, its nearest approach to an industry is stone quarrying. It has only two towns, one of which, Oakham, with a population of just over 3,000, is nearly twice the size of Uppingham, the other. Moreover, it appears always to have had a knack of avoiding the menaces of successive ages. Old Thomas Fuller, the seventeenth-century writer, observed incredulously that 'the county had not one absolute or entire abbey therein. Shew me so fair a bunch of sweet grapes, which had no more flies to suck them.' Again he writes, and hunting people still echo his words, 'No place, so fair for the *Rider*, being more fruitful for the *Abider*.' Yes, the recording of Rutland, even to the very limited extent practised, must be considered (in view of the purposes of the scheme) something of a luxury. But no one who knows the county is likely to complain or to blame.

When, with 1,549 drawings in its portfolio, the scheme came to an end, Leicestershire, Nottinghamshire, and Lincolnshire were among the few counties in which recording had not taken place. So, after Rutland and the next county, Norfolk, there comes a gap in continuity, a jump across the Wash and The Dukeries to Yorkshire and (in the third volume) Derbyshire.

109

TOMBSTONES, HINTON-IN-THE-HEDGES

John Piper

The village which has the good fortune to be known as Hinton-in-the-Hedges lies two miles west of Brackley in the extreme south of Northamptonshire, not far from Oxfordshire and even nearer to Buckinghamshire. It is as quiet as its name, secluded rather than served by narrow roads not yet adapted from, and still given over to, the use of horse-drawn vehicles.

In the long grass of Holy Trinity churchyard are twenty or thirty headstones such as can be found, with a little looking, elsewhere in this corner of the county—of a local type with 'ebullient carving of a specially bold character' of cherubs, skulls, scrolls, festoons of leaves and flowers, shields, panels, and so on. Hardly any names or dates are decipherable or even visible; and this is rather surprising, because the county quarries are famous for stone which, in spite of its soft appearance, seems to have plenty of wear in it.

Until the seventeenth century, although the nobility and gentry might be commemorated inside their local churches in a manner befitting their rank or pretensions, other parishioners ended up beneath grassy mounds outside. During that century the sacred buildings began to suffer infiltration by wealthy tradesmen, but for the most part they, or their relatives, were satisfied to mark their progress and their resting-place with a headstone in the earth. There is a good mural tablet in Holy Trinity bearing the date 1686, but no evidence connects its author with the stones in the churchyard. Just possibly they, or some of them, are the work of one Middleton, a stone-mason of Towcester in the eighteenth century who signs a wall monument of somewhat similar style in the church at Stoke Bruerne. But that guess represents a long shot, and the chances are that these rich and graceful decorations are the product of craftsmen whose fame, even in their lifetime, never extended beyond a few miles. Gloucestershire has, perhaps, the greatest number of these headstones in high relief; but in each county the tradition varies slightly and, slightly or much, the stone also.

COSGROVE

S. R. Badmin, R.W.S.

From Cosgrove one may walk in a few minutes into Buckinghamshire and drive in a few minutes to Gayhurst and find oneself back again in the Cowper country of the first volume.

For the chief feature of Cosgrove's history, and of the picture, we must go back to the poet's last years. An item in the remarkable movement instigated by the Duke of Bridgewater and destined to spread, during the second half of the eighteenth century, a mesh of water-ways all over the country, the Grand Junction Canal was authorized in 1793. It was begun at both ends—at Brentford in Middlesex and at Braunston in Northamptonshire. By 1799 the two halves were about to meet at, or near, Cosgrove, and in fact they met in 1800. But a last-minute suggestion had been made that by means of a high aqueduct a number of locks could be eliminated, and this suggestion, being adopted, had serious results. In the words of Francis Whellan, a county historian of the nineteenth century, the canal was 'carried over the River Ouse and across the long valley to Wolverton, a distance of nearly a mile, by a stupendous embankment'. This aqueduct, he tells us, was originally constructed on arches and was opened on 26 August 1805. The contractors, rather ominously, declined to give more than a twelve months' guarantee, but even that turned out to be far too optimistic. Before the work was completed 'leakages and other indications of instability became apparent, and at length a sudden disruption took place, and inundated the surrounding country'. A solid embankment was substituted for the archways and along it was laid a cast-iron channel, much narrower than the general width of the navigation. The structure, which still exists, was opened to traffic in January 1811.

Mr. Badmin has caught a barge on its way through, or over, the village. In the distance may be seen evidences of a rival service offered by the London Midland and Scottish Railway. When the canal was in course of construction its disconnected stretches were linked by railways. This was before 1800; the trucks were horse-drawn.

STOKE BRUERNE

S. R. Badmin, R.W.S.

On its way to Cosgrove from Blisworth, where there is a branch to Northampton, the old Junction Canal passes through the village of Stoke Bruerne; and here, before Blisworth Tunnel was built, a flight of no fewer than seven locks was constructed, leading down from the south end of the tunnel to the river Tove crossing. Consequently here again, as at Cosgrove, the water-way is above the level of houses in the lower part of the village. It is narrowed by the locks to a width of only 8 or 9 feet.

There was a collapse here, too—not of the canal but of the contractors who were building Blisworth Tunnel. When they went bankrupt in 1797 the company took over the works by direct administration, but its members disagreed on both site and method. Again a firm of contractors was found, and again it 'encountered difficulties' and had to suspend operations. The company itself, achieving harmony through misfortune, then completed and opened the tunnel in March 1805. Another canal system, the Grand Union, also roams the county and, as indicated by the formidable initials on the barge, it has now absorbed the Grand Junction.

Beyond the brick-and-stone bridge the church of St. Mary the Virgin stands, as usual, on the highest available spot. The great days of Stoke Bruerne came in the first half of the seventeenth century. Sir Francis Crane, who with Royal encouragement founded the famous tapestry works at Mortlake, built himself a house at Stoke Bruerne, and there entertained King Charles and Queen Henrietta Maria. Inigo Jones helped him build it and it stood till 1886, when it was almost entirely destroyed by fire.

SCREEN TO RACE-COURSE, TOWCESTER

John Piper

Under National Hunt rules three or four days' racing (discontinued during the war) are held annually at Towcester. Sportsmen attending the meetings pass beneath this triumphal arch, a dignified prelude to their pleasures as well as a screen for their activities.

It was not built for them. It is the entrance from Watling Street to Easton Neston Park, about a mile south-east of the town. The house, which still stands, was designed by Nicholas Hawksmoor, and so were the gardens, but the history of the estate goes back to the reign of Henry VII. In 1527 it was bought by William Fermor, or his brother Richard, Oxfordshire men, and it has remained in the possession of the family ever since.

At Easton Neston, in 1603, James I met Anne of Denmark and Prince Henry on their arrival in England. The present house arose just a hundred years later. It is said to have been begun with two wings designed by Wren, between which Hawksmoor, on the instructions of the first Lord Lempster (or Leominster), inserted a central block in 1702. The house, which was planned to fit the wings, was not helped by their subsequent removal; but it remains a notable creation by an important man.

The subject of Mr. Piper's drawing seems too late for Hawksmoor. Whoever the author, it has an elegant and aristocratic air; and, thanks to the continuity in ownership, the details apply—they were right at the time and they are right now. The Fermor arms—lions' heads—the Fermor crest—a cock's head in a ducal coronet—the Fermor motto—*hora e sempre*—appear above the archway and the semicircular recesses of the wings, together with the expected deer, urns, and other features. Through the wrought-iron gate can be seen the stretches of the park wherein lies, hidden, the house. It is a fine park; one remembers that there is a race-course tucked away in it.

ST. DENIS'S, FAXTON—EXTERIOR

John Piper

'Faxton!' said the farmer in the voice of a man unable to believe his ears. 'Faxton!' He took off his hat; but more was needed and he heaved himself from the driving-seat and stepped out into the fresh air. 'If I wanted to go to Faxton,' he went on very slowly and with evident determination to keep the conversation on rational lines, if that were possible, 'I should take this car home and get out the old pony and bung 'm in the old trap.'

Although Faxton was less than a mile away, the farmer's attitude cannot be called defeatist. It is a difficult place to find and to reach. The main road from Northampton to Market Harborough runs two miles to the west, the Northampton–Kettering road passes on the east; but to Faxton there is no road that remains open. Asking permission from farm to farm, and the way, one trudges to it across fields, amongst cows, and over gates. Faxton itself consists of a few cottages, half a dozen or so, beside a rising green where stands, in the middle, the time-worn, time-honoured church of St. Denis.

It belongs for the most part to the thirteenth century, with traces (as in the north doorway) of the twelfth, as well as of the fourteenth and fifteenth. The most arresting feature in church as in drawing should probably be ascribed to the fifteenth; this is the bell cote with two bells. But the building as a whole is remarkable as one of the very few unrestored churches in this part of the country—an example of Early English altered in the Decorated period and not again. A certain amount of simple repair is now needed if the church is to be saved from the opposing dangers of decay and restoration. It is in the chapelry of Lamport.

ST. DENIS'S, FAXTON—INTERIOR

John Piper

No services have been held here since the autumn of 1939, and the church is kept locked; but dogs give noisy warning of the approach of a stranger and bring out the caretaker and the key from a neighbouring cottage. The dogs are not unfriendly. Nevertheless, visitors who have followed the farmer's advice may be troubled, while in church, by thoughts of the unattended pony in the trap.

The interior, damp and forlorn from disuse, retains its simple beauty. Examples of the carved stone of the capitals and beam-supports can be seen in Mr. Piper's drawing, also one of several memorials of members of the Nicolls family, locally prominent in the sixteenth, seventeenth, and eighteenth centuries. This monument of black and white marble, carved and painted, is to Sir Augustine Nicolls, Kt., who 'having laboured in the high and painful calling of a most revered and just judge for the space of four years fell under the heavy burden at Kendall sitting there Justice of Assize and coming to give judgement upon others, by his comfortable and Christian departure received, we assuredly believe, his judgement with mercy, in the year of our Lord 1616, the third day of August'.

THE PRIORY, WOLLASTON

Michael Rothenstein

With one exception the main features of the quiet villages of Northamptonshire—the thatched or red-tiled roofs, the pleasant yellowish-grey stone—are to be found in the picture of this house. The only one missing is the open view; and that, too, exists in fact, though there is no way of showing it and the house in the same drawing.

Wollaston, close to Wellingborough, the river Nene, and the Bedfordshire border, stands on a modest eminence topped by its church. The Priory is hard by. It is in part brick, in part stone; the near end roofed with red tiles, the far end with thatch; modernized and adapted from century to century to a confusing extent, yet containing portions built 400 years ago and—barring certain features of the much-restored church—older than anything else in the village.

BOUGHTON FROM THE PARK

S. R. Badmin, R.W.S.

The name of Boughton appears twice, and that of Broughton once, in the county guide-books; and so the statement that Mr. Badmin's village lies three miles north of Northampton is no mere conventional murmur of introduction.

It is a pretty place, yet the effect is not entirely serene, is even haunted. It had a fine Decorated church on the green, three-quarters of a mile away, but it crumbled into ruins. The church centred here is, except for the tower, a nineteenth-century building. In the seventeenth and eighteenth centuries, when Greens and Vaux and Wentworths dominated the village at their gates, there was a big house also, but it disappeared long ago from its fashionably absurd park. 'Temples, triumphal arches and artificial ruins', we are told, 'were interspersed in fantastic variety', and it is not necessary to trespass to see, to-day, a dilapidated statue, a broken wall, an arch leading nowhere, and other signs of coldly calculated romanticism. A strip of the castellated wall can be seen in the drawing, as well as an archway which leads somewhere.

Whyte-Melville lived in Boughton and wrote many of his books there.

GRAFTON UNDERWOOD

S. R. Badmin, R.W.S.

This euphoniously named village, a few miles to the north-east of Kettering, is diversified by a duck-supporting stream which runs, like a moat, along the west edge of the roadway. Residents on this side have, when crossing the obstruction, a choice between no fewer than six bridges and a set of stepping-stones.

Apart from the runnel, Grafton Underwood is true to the county type, its houses walled with soft-coloured stone and roofed with thatch or red or grey tiles. These roof materials are used with a pleasant impartiality. For instance, the two projecting houses just above the left corner of the first bridge are thatched, though their neighbours are tiled; whilst the small building in the foreground on the right has its near end tiled, its lower half thatched.

BULWICK

S. R. Badmin, R.W.S.

From within or from without, Mr. Badmin made drawings of fifteen Northampton-shire villages, seven of which are reproduced in these pages. The pleasant-coloured stone, the thatched roofs, and other characteristics of the main streets have already been mentioned more than once. Here is a village shown in its setting. Once dense with the trees of the ancient and royal forest of Rockingham, the gentle swell of the ground now lies revealed. The view may be compared with that at Colly Weston, a few miles to the north, where a rather sharper rise and fall announces the nearness of Rutlandshire.

The forest was divided into three districts or bailiwicks—a word easily corrupted into Bulwick. The Perpendicular tower and spire are the best features of the restored church of St. Nicholas, dominating the peaceful scene.

Berwick   J. R. Bach

INN SIGNS, UPPINGHAM

Barbara Jones

The signboards of inns have their ups and downs. Nowadays, serious writers find them worthy of attention, and there are places where art students may practise their design.

The signs shown here are not of the more common, swinging kind. The unicorn, painted white, gorged with a red coronet with a black chain attached thereto, arrests us at the doorway of an old hostelry in the High Street. The carving of the arms of the Marquess of Exeter, whose family seat is at Burghley House, Stamford, a few miles away, makes an impressive vignette, but in fact is borne by one of the smallest public houses imaginable. During the seventy-five years that have passed since it was cut, the stone has weathered very agreeably, lending the sign all the dignity of a lineage stretching back to Queen Elizabeth's Lord High Treasurer.

Uppingham rejoices in well-named inns, and these two signs are not the only ones in relief. The fine sundial above the unicorn is very 'Rutland'; the little county is full of these old aids to punctuality.

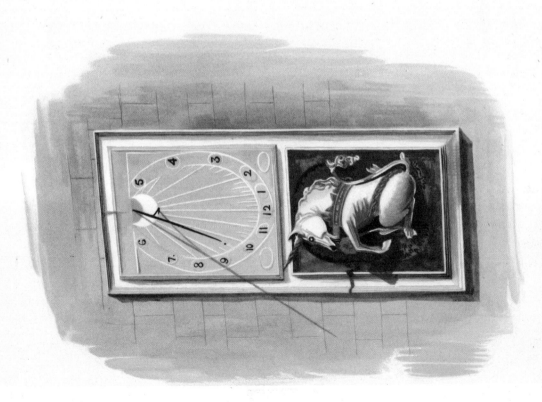

"The Unicorn" High St.

"Exeter Arms."

Ian Sayer, Uppingham.
Bodmin Jones 1943.

CHURCH INSTRUMENTS, RIDLINGTON

Barbara Jones

At the west end of SS. Mary Magdalene and Andrew's hangs a case of musical instruments used, up to 1860, by the Ridlington Church orchestra to accompany the singing. Such bands were once common; organs took a long time to dwindle to a size and price suited to a village church. The invention of the harmonium at Copenhagen in 1779 revealed possibilities which, explored and embedded in numerous patents, led to the substitution of one musician for six or ten. The organist's greater control of the service was considered, at the time, gain unalloyed.

A few orchestras lasted till 1870, but the experience of Ridlington was probably nearer the normal. Again, no fixed instrumental balance can be laid down. At Ridlington the woodwind—2 oboes, a bassoon, and a flute—must have overwhelmed the solitary fiddle, but (as readers of *Under the Greenwood Tree* will recall) this arrangement would not have found favour at Mellstock.

'I can well bring back to my mind,' said Mr. Penny, 'what I said to poor Joseph Ryme (who took the tribble part in Chalk-Newton Church for two-and-forty year) when they thought of having clar'nets there. "Joseph," I said, says I, "depend upon 't, if so be you have them tooting clar'nets you'll spoil the whole set-out. Clar'nets were not made for the service of the Lard; you can see it by looking at 'em," I said. And what cam o't? Why, souls, the parson set up a barrel-organ on his own account within two years o' the time I spoke, and the old choir went to nothing.'

'Robert Penny, you was in the right,' broke in the eldest Dewey. 'They should ha' stuck to strings. Your brass-man is a rafting dog—well and good; your reed-man is a dab at stirring ye—well and good; your drum-man is a rare bowel-shaker—good again. But I don't care who hears me say it, nothing will speak to your heart wi' the sweetness o' the man of strings!'

Hardy was born in 1840. In 1896, in a preface for a new edition of his novel, then 24 years old, he makes it clear that he had relied on memories of the west-gallery musicians of his childhood, of 1850 at latest. 'Fiddle-strings, rosin and music-paper', he tells us, 'were supplied by a pedlar, who travelled exclusively in such wares from choir to choir, coming to each village about every six months. Tales are told of the consternation once caused among the church fiddlers when . . . he did not come in time, owing to being snowed up on the downs, and the straits they were in through having to make shift with whipcord and twine for strings.'

Barbara Jones 1943
Ridlington Church . Rutland

THE MILL, DUDDINGTON

S. R. Badmin, R.W.S.

Duddington is a village on the Northamptonshire bank of the river Welland, which here serves as the county boundary with Rutlandshire.

Its old water-mill, its ancient and ill-restored four-arched bridge, its church and picturesque houses have gained for it a local reputation which sometimes reaches the ears of tourists and tempts them to visit it; but more often people come upon it unprepared as they travel along the Uppingham–Peterborough road. Without any notable history to lend it adventitious aid, it is simply a beautiful village, and there is really nothing else to be said half as interesting as what Mr. Badmin has to say on the page opposite.

COLLY WESTON

S. R. Badmin, R.W.S.

The last and most northerly in Mr. Badmin's series of pictures of Northamptonshire villages, Colly Weston (or Collyweston, or Colley Weston), lies in the quarrying area. The history of the local quarry goes back to very early times, and countless buildings in the east and east-midland counties carry the slates of Colly Weston in their roofs. Geologically speaking, the bed belongs to the Inferior Oolite and lies at the base of the so-called Lincolnshire limestone. It has proved rich in fossils.

Only six miles to the north-east is Barnack, whence came, until the exhaustion of the quarries some four hundred years ago, the finest building stone in the country.

Colly Weston, however, was recorded not for industrial reasons but as a type. Modest as its houses are, they—like the houses in so many other villages of the county—are made of the best materials in England. It has the usual view, or even a little better, for here, though the address is still Northamptonshire, the slight increase in the rise and fall of the landscape proclaims the imminence of Rutland.

J. R. Badmin. Lithographer

ST. MATTHEW'S, NORMANTON

John Piper

Numerous and resounding essays, political, economic, and social, as well as architectural, could be hung about this church. Surrounded by a medieval village a medieval church, probably of the fourteenth century, once stood on the site. By 1579 it was reported to be in ruinous condition, but it survived in some sort of shape till 1764. In that year, a tremendous year, a year from which the neighbourhood has never yet recovered, Sir Gilbert Heathcote, 3rd baronet, swept away church, village, and parish in order to encompass Normanton Hall with an adequate park. So thoroughly did he carry out his purpose that, save for the rectory and two or three houses, the parish outside the park remains empty of habitations. The population at the last census was forty-one.

For the spiritual needs of his family, staff, and guests Sir Gilbert provided a plain building in a style described as 'Italian of the most unpretending character', though the old bell-turret seems to have been kept. This, too, disappeared in 1826 when, above a new western vestibule and portico, a new tower arose—a slightly elongated copy of the four towers which, a hundred years earlier, Thomas Archer had added to his church of St. John the Evangelist in Smith Square, Westminster, in the hope of correcting the results of subsidence. St. John's suffered severely from the German bombers and three of its towers have gone. The fourth, however, is reasonably whole, so that when the work of restoration begins it may not be necessary, after all, to fetch the details back again from Rutland.

Meanwhile the Heathcote baronets were progressively becoming Barons Willoughby de Eresby, Barons Aveland, and Earls of Ancaster, and as a memorial to one of their number the eighteenth-century nave and chancel were pulled down and reconstructed in harmony with the alterations of 1826. As far as its external, Classic-Renaissance appearance is concerned the story ends here, but the adventures of the church were not yet over. The big house, built by Sir Gilbert's father or grandfather on the fashionable model of the time, with a central block and extended arms, and subsequently modified by Sir Robert Taylor working in the Adam style —the big mansion was sold in 1925 and taken down, taken away. Nothing remains beyond parts of outbuildings; and St. Matthew's, having lost house, lords, ladies, and domestics, stands isolated in the park that was once a village.

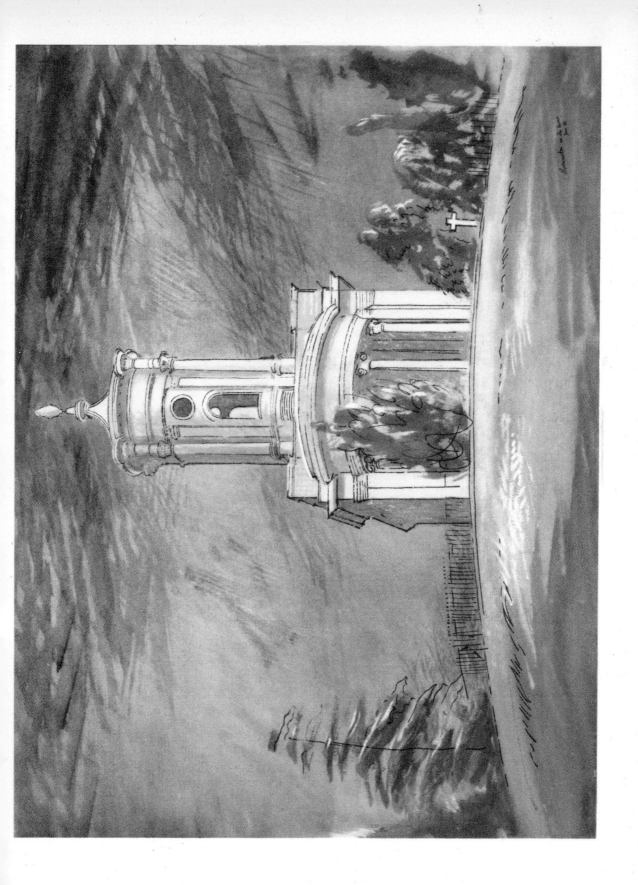

BUTTER CROSS, OAKHAM

Barbara Jones

'Market Crosses', wrote John Britton, in his *Architectural Antiquities of Great Britain*, 'are of various shapes and sizes, and all appear to have been erected for the threefold object of administering to the luxuries of monachism, disseminating the Catholic religion, and promoting traffic. In almost every town that had an abbey, or any other religious foundation, there was one of these structures, where farmers and other persons, from the neighbouring villages and hamlets, resorted, on stated days, to exhibit and sell their eggs, fowls, grain, and other provisions. At most markets and fairs it was then customary (as it is still) to pay certain tolls on articles sold. Many of these tolls belonged to the monasteries. . . . To increase these, and, at the same time, propagate the sacred doctrines of Catholicism, we are informed, by several ancient writers, that the monks frequently harangued the populace from these crosses.'

This well-known, one may almost say this standard, description has been quoted rather to place the subject in its setting than because of its strict applicability to Oakham. The Butter Cross, which cannot be earlier than the end of the sixteenth century, came too late for the monks; and even if it had a predecessor, Oakham never had abbeys. In 1390 a William Dalby founded the Hospital of St. John; he also founded a Priory of St. Anne of Coventry; but these possible clues would lead us far afield.

The very clear picture on the opposite page leaves little need of description. However, it may be worth observing that the central pier is of stone whereas the eight posts at the angles of the roof are of timber on stone bases. The three steps round the main octagonal shaft may have been used as a rostrum; they certainly formed seats for the occupants of the stocks. Whether the fifth hole in the beam is a sign of a light sentence, with only one leg held, or of shortage of wood seems to be a matter of doubt. The four-sided sundial and vane should be noted. It is known that there were four other crosses at Oakham, probably serving to mark boundaries. This, the only survivor, is an example of the simpler kind of market centre, making no attempt to compete with the elaborately decorated affairs at places like Chichester and Malmesbury.

BURLEY-ON-THE-HILL

Barbara Jones

On the demolition of Normanton, Burley-on-the-Hill became 'the lordliest residence in the county of Rutland'. It has always, thanks to its magnificent site overlooking the Vale of Catmose, been the most conspicuous; from the roof, the view extends to five counties. Guide-books warn the visitor not to confuse it with Burghley House, ten miles away, but suggest no means of avoiding confusion.

There had long been a great house on the site when, very early in the seventeenth century, James I was the guest here of Sir John Harington. It was an eventful stay. His Majesty, a keen but clumsy rider, fell off his horse and was so bruised that, on leaving, he had to travel by coach; and a little later Sir John sold the place to the Royal favourite, George ('Steenie') Villiers, Duke of Buckingham. He pulled the old house down and built an immense mansion with (according to Fuller's *Worthies*) stables 'where horses (if their *pabulum* so plenty as their *stabulum* stately) were the best accommodated in England'. For a few years there were great goings-on. To enliven a house party which included Charles I, the dwarf Jeffery Hudson was served at table in a cold pie; and Ben Jonson's masque, *The Gypsies*, was given its first performance, all the actors being noblemen. But this house, like its owner, did not last long. In 1645 a small garrison of Roundheads, being threatened by stronger Royalist forces, set fire to the buildings as they decamped.

The stables remained, and they affected the design of the present house. This was built fifty years later (1694–1702) by Daniel Finch, 2nd Earl of Nottingham—a man, according to Macaulay, with complexion 'so dark that he might have passed for a native of a warmer climate than ours; and his harsh features were composed to an expression resembling that of a chief mourner'. He was known as Don Dismallo, and he owned a number of houses, none of which seems to have satisfied him. He had already sold his Kensington residence to William III, who turned it into Kensington Palace, when (so the story goes) he saw by chance, while riding to York, the splendid ruins of Burley. Like several of his friends, such as Sir John Lowther, he seems to have been his own architect. He used the fashionable model of a central block with arms which he exaggerated to a fabulous length. They have been ridiculed by later generations as a Folly; but Defoe, seeing the place when new, declared that 'I do not know a House in *Britain*, which excels all the rest in so many particulars'. In 1796 the design was modified, not without ruthlessness, by Repton.

Battersea Park, from the River Thames, circa 1862

NORFOLK

Artists

FRANK EMANUEL   BARBARA JONES   RUSSELL REEVE

MARTIN HARDIE, C.B.E.   JULIAN LEATHART   R. L. YOUNG

MONA MOORE

FOR such flat country, the features of Norfolk are surprisingly varied. By no means all are represented in the following pages, or in the collection itself. The sandy margin was seldom recorded, and never at those points where large hotels and golf courses have brought renown. The quiet of the bird-nesting sanctuaries was respected, and the yachting centres on the Broads were likewise omitted, though for a different reason—records of them by scores of hard-worked brushes appear annually in the galleries of dealers and societies. As in other coastal counties, many characteristic inland villages had to be neglected, too, because in the years when recording was being done they were in less danger from foe and friend than the places nearer the sea. But the wild Breckland, the home of rabbits and flint-knappers, on the Suffolk border; the equally wild and still bleaker country lining The Wash; sundry aspects of the historic towns of Yarmouth, Norwich, and King's Lynn—these were recorded together with, as in Essex and Suffolk, an unusually high percentage of churches.

In the accompanying notes a few salient features are indicated, but even without the historical digressions it would not have been possible to do justice either to the peculiarities of East Anglian churches (flint and stone panelling, known as flush-work; circular towers; &c.) or to the impression which they make in areas where their superb forms meet the eye as regularly as milestones. They must be visited, and with a guide-book.

Marshland, on the short Lincolnshire border, holds the finest group, but up and down the eastern counties there are districts where the churches, as beautiful and as thick on the ground, are inferior only in size. They are apt to be ignored by the wandering artist who has to consider means of paying for his holiday, they are seldom the subject of casual recording; and of planned recording there has never been enough, or anything like enough, even when there has been any. Good starting places for such recording abound, and the churches of East Anglia are one of the best of them.

SOUTH QUAY, GREAT YARMOUTH

Mona Moore

'Yarmouth is a sweet place indeed,' wrote the Rev. James Woodforde, 'the key is very fine.' The eupeptic divine was enchanted by everything he saw, including 'the German Ocean, out of which I drank'.

That was in 1775; and since his day some millions of visitors have endorsed his views on the resort, if not on refreshment. The 'very fine key'—North Quay, Hall Quay, and especially South Quay—was, when first constructed, reckoned superior to all the quays of Europe, Rotterdam, Antwerp, Marseilles, Bordeaux, Lisbon, and the rest, with the single exception of Seville. Such a claim can no longer be made, but the broad mile of eighteenth-century houses, roadway, trucks, hawsers, and gangways beside the Yare presents a beautiful and animated scene, suggesting at times a smaller Amsterdam or Rouen. Ruskin, if it would be misleading to say that he mentioned them in the same breath, once linked Yarmouth and Venice in the same sentence. There are over 23,000 yards of quay, and up to a limit of about 800 tons several hundred vessels can be accommodated.

Here, far from the piers and the promenade, the sands and the cinemas, is a Yarmouth full of interest, history, and ships in the anchorage. By ferrying over this estuary and cutting across this quay, David Copperfield shortened his journeys between Blundeston (Blunderstone) and Peggotty's boat. Many heads have been thrust through these windows to watch Nelson walk by. On 6 November 1800, two years to a day after the Battle of the Nile, he landed at Yarmouth accompanied by the Hamiltons and awaited by a censorious Admiralty, an indignant wife, and an adoring populace. Four months later he was again at Yarmouth and after another four months returned there, having fought in the meantime the furious fight at Copenhagen. But these are the memories, fictitious or real, of yesterday. Five hundred years before these houses were built Henry III granted the town the right to call itself Great, in distinction from Yarmouth in the Isle of Wight. His father before him, King John, bestowed a charter in exchange for a perpetual payment of £55 a year. In 1946 a good story was provided for the local press by the discovery that this recognition of the privileges enjoyed as free borough was still being paid, to an insurance company. The money was collected by the Crown until the time of Charles II; but (pending a fuller statement) the suggestion seemed to be that that experienced monarch, recognizing a realizable asset when he saw one, . . .

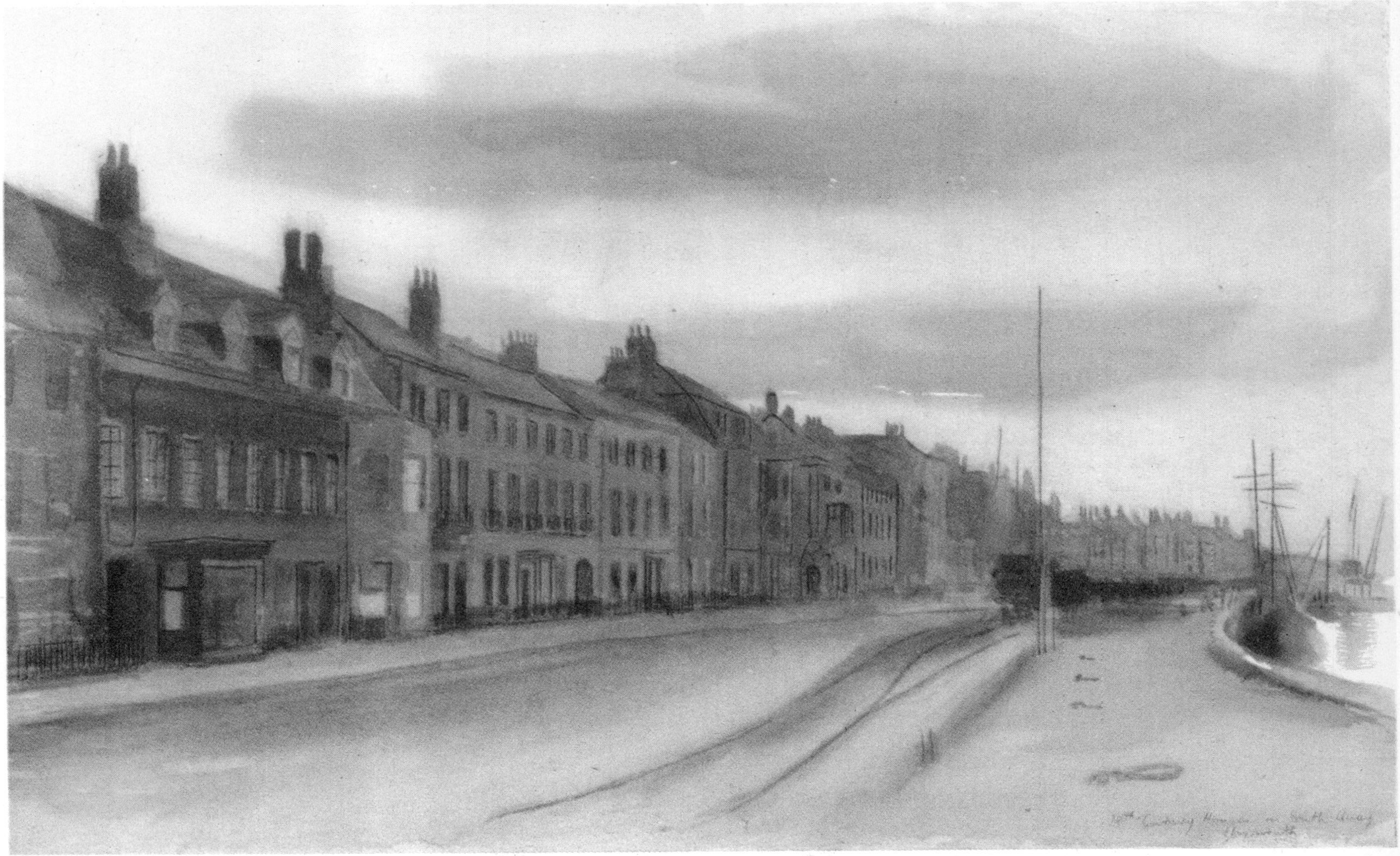

A ROW, GREAT YARMOUTH

Frank Emanuel

All fishing-ports are addicted to slim passage-ways between the houses, but none
has ever been found to compare in this respect with Yarmouth. The town lies on
a narrow tongue of land tapering from north to south, like a smaller Manhattan,
and along this run five streets parallel to the quays. Defoe's description, written in
1724, is still wonderfully applicable: 'The Streets are all exactly strait from North
to South, with Lanes or Alleys, which they call *ROWS*, crossing them in strait lines
also from East to West; so that it is the most regular built Town in *England,* and
seems to have been built all at once. Or, that the Dimensions of the Houses, and
the Extent of the Streets, were laid out by Consent.' The frequency of the alleys
is such that, for a mile or more, the houses are usually in pairs. In 1940 there were
145 rows. Little more than half that number are now recognizable and habitable.
The old fishing-harbour suffered severely from enemy bombers who, singly or in
small formations, found it easy to reach and still easier to describe as an important
naval base.

The widest of the rows is 6 feet across, the narrowest 29 inches; and special
vehicles had to be designed to serve them—long, slender carts with two small
wheels beneath the body, 'a sort of horse wheelbarrow'. They were invented late
in the fifteenth century and (perhaps in honour of the reigning monarch, Henry VII)
were called Harry Carriers and were driven by Harry Carmen. At other times they
have gone by other names—trolls, trolleys, Yarmouth carts, and Yarmouth coaches.

FISHERMEN'S ALMSHOUSE, GREAT YARMOUTH

Mona Moore

'An Hospital', runs the rectangular notice over the archway, 'for Decayed Fishermen, founded by the Corporation in 1702.' Elsewhere, in an oval frame, are the regulations painted on a board 250 years ago. Decay was reasonably assumed at sixty; and a fisherman who had attained that age was eligible and so was his wife, however far she might be from rotting. If he became a widower he was free to marry again within the hospital (it is not explained how he would find a bride there), but if he chose his new partner from outside she had to be approved by the Committee. That a salted bachelor of sixty, noting the first symptoms of decay, might feel it time to settle down was a possibility that seems not to have been envisaged.

Some fifteen or sixteen little houses surround the courtyard, but two of them are half-demolished by a bomb deliberately aimed, in the belief of the inmates, at the brewery across the road. Inside their enclosure the old men like to gather, when the weather is kind, and seat themselves on benches with their backs to the wall, there to exchange gossip and grievances, to smoke their pipes, sun themselves, and watch the world—a world of fish eaters—going by on Church Plain; until distant cries, shrill or faded, call them back and they roll away each to his own doorway, to the welcoming smell of his own bloater.

In the centre of this prettiest of retreats stands a beset matron not hard to identify as Charity. The figure sheltering beneath the cupola might suitably have been St. Nicholas, since he is the patron saint not only of sailors but also of the celebrated parish church a few steps distant. Against this facile supposition, hagiographers are agreed in pronouncing the likeness to be that of St. Peter; and no doubt we are safe in their hands.

Fishermans Alms H.
Gt Yarmouth

ST. PETER MANCROFT, NORWICH, FROM BETHEL STREET

Russell Reeve

Norwich contains thirty-seven old churches, not counting the Cathedral; and in this respect, though there are some forty larger cities in England, it is surpassed by London only. Moreover, Norwich is exceptionally fortunate in the quality of the bells hung in its churches. Anyone who cares to sit in the Market Place at half-past ten on a sunny Sunday morning may enjoy a memorable experience. The warm air seems translated into music.

At the raised south-west corner of the square, where Bethel Street enters it, stands the parish church of St. Peter Mancroft. The site, on which an earlier church was built by the Normans, was the great meadow attached to the castle, the *magna crofta*; and it is of this that the name Mancroft is a corruption. The Norman church, having fallen into disrepair, was (in the graceful phrase of our day) scheduled for demolition in 1390, but the first stone of the existing church was not laid for another forty years. Completion and consecration took place in 1455. On two if not three occasions it underwent restoration in Victorian times.

How high the tower is, where to look for the grave and monuments of Sir Thomas Browne, what the vestry contains, and which architectural features are characteristic of Norfolk perpendicular—all this and much more can be found in any reputable guide-book as well as in the leaflets obtainable in the church itself. But what, for one reason or another, nobody mentions is the change that has recently befallen the setting of the old church. Mr. Reeve has drawn it from an angle where it still has the quality of dominance that used to belong to it. Had he drawn it from the east or north side of the Market Place, he would have been compelled to show it utterly dwarfed by the City Hall, erected in 1938. Such changes in proportion are common enough to-day, and are perhaps none the better for being as a rule so gradual as to pass unnoticed by almost everybody. Here the whole outlook, the very bearings of the central square, were altered at one blow. The church which, from the conformation of the ground and from its own virtues, drew all eyes to itself now stands suddenly shrunken beside the palace of the City Fathers. Even people who have come specially to see the church cannot give it their immediate attention. Even those who do not admire the City Hall find it impossible to postpone that building to their second glance.

ST. MARY THE VIRGIN'S, GREAT HAUTBOIS

R. L. Young

Visitors who find themselves in the Broadland area of Norfolk and inquire the way to Hautbois will not, especially the musical ones, receive much help; and if, nevertheless, they reach the village, they will meet with little response to a mention of St. Mary the Virgin's. Yet both church and village are well known for miles around, and there is a way of making local faces lighten, if only the stranger has the knack. It is very easy. He asks for St. Tebbald's of Hobbies.

The church was dedicated to the Blessed Virgin, but it contained a statue of St. Theobald standing in a chapel sacred to him; and as this image was credited with miraculous powers and drew hundreds of pilgrims to the shrine every year, in time the original designation was forgotten and people grew to believe that the church was St. Theobald's. For some reason or other—perhaps the distance of the church from the village and the several alternatives available in a neighbourhood very well stocked with places of worship—the old flint and stone building, Norman and Gothic, was allowed to fall into disrepair. It continued to be used until well into the nineteenth century, but with increasing difficulty; and eventually a rector, Mr. Girling, in 1863 built a new and nearer church, largely at his own expense. The good clergyman has been blamed for its inferiority to the old church; but for neither the neglect of St. Mary's nor the shortcomings of mid-Victorian architects can he be held responsible.

St. Mary's is now a ruin, a beautiful and peaceful ruin standing amid fields a mile outside the village. Its circular tower may be compared with the similar tower at Little Saling, illustrated in the Essex section of this volume. The south porch and the walls of the nave are still in existence; then follows an open gap; and then comes the chancel, roofed in and used as a mortuary chapel. People are still buried there, and their graves are in the grassy aisles, for the overgrown churchyard is full—full of good examples of nineteenth-century tombstones, some high, some barely level with the grass, and some perhaps sunk below earth level. Certain names, recurring, mark the old families of the village—Gant, Hallock, Fitt, Lee—names such as Gray read at Stoke Poges.

WALPOLE ST. PETER

Barbara Jones

Walpole is a small place with several claims to fame. It gave its name to one of the great families of England. Again, 'at a place called Cross Keys, in this parish, is a passage over the Washes, for horses and carriages, to Long Sutton, in Lincolnshire', and it was at this dangerous ford that King John, losing his baggage and very nearly his life, bequeathed a stir of excitement to generations of schoolchildren. Lastly, Walpole possesses a church whose magnificence has slowly eclipsed those other memories until, to-day, it is the main, if not the sole, attraction for visitors.

Besides being one of the finest perpendicular churches in the country, it contains many features of unusual beauty. Across the west end stretches a wooden Jacobean screen; and after passing through this one finds oneself amid fine benches of carved oak. The chancel screen dates from the time of 'the royal saint', Henry VI, and consists of twelve painted panels of saints—Catherine, the Blessed Virgin, Margaret, John the Evangelist, James, Thomas, Peter, Paul, Andrew, Mary Magdalene, Dorothea, and Barbara—each beneath a canopy. Farther east still the altar rises at the top of a steep flight of ten steps, made necessary by the tunnel connecting the northern and southern sides of the churchyard. Enumeration of points worth noting is as easily continued as curtailed; but they can be found in the guide-books, and though, when they have all been listed, they may draw the antiquarian, they will hardly prepare the ordinary visitor for the charm of the place. The exterior can be studied in Miss Jones's painting. The interior, in detail and as a whole, is no less impressive.

Walpole St. Peter, Norfolk.

Drawn from nature 1912

MILL, WALPOLE HIGHWAY

Barbara Jones

As may be guessed from its trim appearance (compare it with the tower mill at Great Bardfield in Essex), this is one of the mills, a dwindling number, still in use. The miller has a supplementary steam-engine, which allows work to continue on such windless days as occur beside The Wash as well as during those more frequent spells when half a gale blows. Nevertheless, this is the oldest tower mill (1743) in operation by wind in England. It has been rebuilt, perhaps twice, and slightly raised in height, and much of its gear is of modern design. It belongs to the West Norfolk type, favouring the South Lincolnshire and Cambridgeshire practice.

More reasons than one account for the disuse of windmills—to be precise, three main reasons. First, the irregular hours, very protracted when the wind is suitable, and much hanging about, doing nothing, when it is absent or too strong. Workmen like reliable hours, and for a long time now young men have avoided jobs in windmills. Secondly, windmills grind whole meal only, whereas the public prefers bread made of white flour. Chicken meal and other animal foods offer a fair market, but it is hardly enough to maintain the necessary turnover. Lastly, while earnings have dropped, costs have risen, especially the costs of repair. Reliable authorities estimate that there are not six millwrights left in the country; and so, when the services of one are needed, the miller is apt to be faced by a long wait and a heavy additional charge for travelling expenses.

A note that has become rather general in character offers opportunity for a word on the origin of windmills. In the sixty-first chapter of his *Decline and Fall of the Roman Empire* the historian asserts, in one of his magisterial asides, that the first windmills were in 'the dry country of Asia Minor', and that the method was noted and introduced into Europe by a Crusader. Since Gibbon's death other voices have been heard, some giving the credit to the Greeks of the first and second centuries A.D., others to an anonymous inventor of western Europe. Windmills seem to have reached Normandy and Britain early in the twelfth century.

Wispele Mill . N. Wisbech   Barbara Jones 1942

ST. MARY'S, WEST WALTON—THE BELL TOWER

Barbara Jones

If slightly less splendid than St. Peter's at Walpole, St. Mary's would be remarkable enough in a district where it was not called upon to compete with the other six churches of Marshland.

It was built in the middle of the thirteenth century, in the Early English style; and, as for some of the old houses in Lynn, the stone used was brought down the Welland and the Nene from Barnack in Northamptonshire. The feature shown here is not unique in Marshland, for there is a detached belfry at Terrington also. At Walton it stands just the length of a cricket pitch (22 yds.) south of the somewhat diminished church, and serves as a formal and imposing entrance to the churchyard. Once, it is said, a leaden-covered spire sprang from the tower, but there is no visible trace of it now. Although the path beneath the wooden roof is a single one, the arches of the tower are open on all four sides. The niches, designed for saints and apostles, are empty, or would be empty were it not for the dwarf bushes of elder-berry, sustaining life on a sparse diet all over the walls. Their green leaves can be seen, pale against the stone, dark against the sky, to within a few feet of the summit.

The seven noble churches of Marshland—Clenchwarton (St. Margaret's), Tilney All Saints', Terrington St. Clement's, Walsoken (All Saints'), Emneth (St. Edmund's), Walpole St. Peter's, and West Walton (St. Mary's)—stand in a fertile, level area between the Great Ouse and the Nene rivers. This area, seven miles by fourteen, is part of the low-lying fen country at the junction of Norfolk, Lincolnshire, Huntingdonshire, and Cambridgeshire. The reclamation (of Marshland and the adjoining part known as South Holland where, until the seventeenth and eighteenth centuries, men lived amphibious lives) belongs to the endless, complex story of the fens—the story of a struggle which, with many reverses, disappointments, and interruptions, began in the days of the Romans and still continues.

West Walton Church, Nr Wisbech.   Richin Tower 1842

SAVAGE'S YARD, KING'S LYNN

Barbara Jones

After alluding to Dr. Burney's tenure of the post of organist to St. Margaret's Church, Baedeker goes on to note, in one of his happier association of ideas, that 'a special industry of Lynn is the manufacture of merry-go-rounds'. Savage's Yard is the headquarters of this trade, or was; for the roundabouts have lost something of their hold on it, and less voluptuous types of engineering now prevail. But here and there, in corners, items of the old traffic still linger, a set of horses in for repair, or a damaged organ—the very one, it may be, that long ago, when almost new, was shown to the gentleman from Leipzig and formed the subject of the second entry made that day in his note-book under the letter 'O'.

The horse in the picture is only very lightly carved about the head and saddle, with all the rest of the decoration painted *trompe l'œil* to imitate carving; it is probably an inner-circle horse, counterfeiting more cheaply the magnificence of the outer animals. Lying in the foreground is a length of organ music with slits for notes, rather like a pianola roll but folded zigzag on card. The two figures standing on the organ are the bandsmen, automata who strike at bells or little drums in time to the music. They are usually in sharp contrast to the rest of the machine, for where the animals prance glittering in the lights on Bank Holiday evenings and are inlaid with mirrors and highly varnished, the music makers are plump and unsparkling, with the strained gaze of men who feel their position.

A view of the world-wide industry is obtainable from one of the old catalogues. In 1902 (that happy year when war was followed by peace, no other alternative occurring to anyone) the firm had been established for over half a century, and during that time had 'patented and placed upon the market all the principal novelties that have delighted the many thousands of pleasure seekers at home and abroad. . . . The illustrations . . . only portray a few of the machines.' The introduction is followed by twenty pages illustrating the few—Excelsior World-Famed Poultry, Switchback Galloping Horses ('Ostriches or Cockerels fitted if desired'), a Colonial Racing Stud, the Sea-On-Land which simulated the rocking of a boat at sea, superb organs, brassy steam engines, and fantastic animals. At the end is the telegraphic code for orders from abroad, with the help of which anyone, by scribbling ELOTE ORESTES TRAVELLER TENTIAL TRUMPET on a cable form, could set a flock of switchback flying ostriches winging their way from Norfolk to Chile.

THE DUKE'S HEAD HOTEL, KING'S LYNN

Mona Moore

Of the many splendours of Lynn, Tuesday Market Place is perhaps the noblest; and of the buildings surrounding this fine square none catches the eye sooner than *The Duke's Head*. Henry Bell, a local architect, designed it for John Turner, whose family 'bore great sway in the town for a whole century'. An older inn, *The Gryffyn*, was standing on the site when Turner decided to buy it, pull it down, and replace it by something larger and more up to date. He was not in the hotel business, but he successfully followed the adjoining trade of vintner; and it is untrue that (as one chronicler has stated) he built it as a family mansion. The story that the choice of title was determined by his admiration for James, Duke of York, also has a doubtful air. By the time the hotel was opened, in 1689, James had ceased to be a duke and become a king; had ceased to be a reigning king and become a king in exile. Few prosperous wine merchants would go out of their way to flaunt disloyalty to a new, suspicious, and well-informed ruler.

In the appearance of the house the principal change was effected by a plasterer who buried the old brickwork beneath an irremovable paste. The existing entrance, if an adaptation, does not seriously disturb the design. The Turner arms can be seen above the central pediment.

Snobbery takes different forms in different generations. The hotel prospered, and during the long ascendancy of the great Whig families in the eighteenth century it was worth the landlord's while to see his premises (built by old Turner 'as an inn for the accommodation of merchants resorting to the Exchange') used as the party headquarters and to admit canvassers, agents, supporters, and all the rabble of electioneering. But even when, in 1791, a London coach started outside the door every Tuesday, Thursday, and Sunday, *The Duke's Head* took pride in being no mere coaching inn. It was not good business, not high-class business, to accept clients off the public coach. A hired post-chaise was tolerated, but only private carriages with crests on the panels were well and truly welcomed. The occupants were helped to earth and, without filling up a form, conducted to the Boston, Newcastle, London, Hare, Hound, Fox, Partridge, or Cockfighting chamber.

A HOUSE, KING'S LYNN

Barbara Jones

That unsuccessful, dauntless agriculturist, Arthur Young, stopped at *The Duke's Head* in 1768 and found it 'exceeding civil and reasonable'. On leaving the building he must have turned, at least on one occasion, to the right, for he cast a lacklustre eye on Henry Bell's masterpiece, the Market Cross, which stood, until it was demolished in 1826, on the north side of Tuesday Market Place. 'It is not heavy,' he observed, 'and that is all I can say for it.'

Even if he noticed the house standing behind the Cross, on the site of the old Town Wall, he did not see the façade here depicted. This decorators' riot is of much later date—possibly about 1865, when the premises were adapted by the firm of timber merchants carrying on business there to-day. For the first 200 years of its life the house may have been a wine merchant's. The spacious cellars, still in existence, are not uncommon in Lynn, which was for long the third principal harbour (after London and Bristol) for Rhenish, port, and other wines; and if the old house was a vintner's the evidence consists less, perhaps, in the cellars than in the new frontage. The black dots which form the centres and corners of the circles, squares, triangles, lozenges, and diagonals of the geometrical extravaganza are the bases of port-wine bottles projecting from the plaster. They could be happy mementoes of buying or of selling; but a mere consumer, even if he found no difficulty in supplying the empties, might hesitate at studding his walls with his weakness.

The house, visible from a long way down the High Street, has a gaily, a wildly irresponsible air, contrasting pleasantly or unpleasantly with the proper subjects of these volumes. In the life of artist and committee, its recording marked a rare moment of relaxation.

PATRICK & THOMPSON
TIMBER YARD & SAW MILLS

House in the Square, King Lynn
Drawn June 1842

THE CUSTOM HOUSE, KING'S LYNN

Mona Moore

Whatever the merits of his vanished Market Cross, Henry Bell's chief remaining work is the Custom House. Though standing very handily for its needs on Purfleet Quay, it was not designed as a douane. Early in 1682 Bell's patron, Alderman John Turner (later, being Sir John, he was responsible for the arrest of Eugene Aram), directed the attention of the Council to the lack of a central meeting-place for merchants, traders, and business men of all kinds, and offered to pay for a suitable building if the Corporation would grant a site. The suggestion was approved, Bell was commissioned, and in 1683 the Exchange (or Exchequer) arose. From the first the upper floor seems to have been rented by the Customs officers, and four years after Sir John's death in 1711 his nephew sold the building (without query if it was his to sell) to the Government as a Custom House. It still fulfils this purpose very adequately; but at the end of the eighteenth century, when the annual duties at Lynn exceeded those of all ports except London, Bristol, Liverpool, and Hull, it must have been a little small for the business.

It is a charming and characteristic structure of freestone, in the Renaissance style, with a tier of Ionic above a tier of Doric pilasters. The pyramidical roof mounts to a small, open turret topped by a pinnacle. In the original design the ground archways were unclosed and the cupola was higher, but these variations seem never to have taken shape, and the building was erected as it is to-day. The carved heads above the arches and similar heads in the hall of *The Duke's Head* must have been executed by the same hand.

A little shuffling about, a little peering up at the statue over the north door is recommended. It represents Charles II, and may be the work of C. G. Cibber; it must have been done, by whatever sculptor, between 1683, when the house was built, and 1685, when the King died. As a portrait it bears so close a resemblance to the bust (in the Victoria and Albert Museum) made by Honoré Pelle in 1684 as to leave us in no doubt of what the King looked like when he was 54. Pouting with satiation and disillusionment, his furrowed face seems to express an over-mastering incredulity even of his own motives. But almost in spite of himself his charm lingers; indeed, his very contempt for it, his weariness of exerting it, gives it a final twist.

CLIFTON'S HOUSE, KING'S LYNN

Barbara Jones

Though it passes a stiffish test in being one of the show places of Lynn, the house is merely a very old house, with a history that is long rather than full. Walter Besant chose it as the home of his heroine in *The Lady of Lynn*, but even that industrious writer found nothing to say about it.

At the bottom of the garden stands a wing of a late-sixteenth-century building with a high brick tower, part of the original residence of an important local family named Thoresby. Very early in the eighteenth century its owner was Samuel Taylor. He, like John Turner, was a wealthy wine merchant (wholesale or retail, the town must have been full of them; by the time the three-bottle habit had trained the English gentleman to his highest peak of fitness, nearly a quarter of a million gallons of wine, most of it port, were passing annually through the customs at Lynn), and when he decided to give the house a new front he, too, employed Bell. At least, it is generally thought, if not positively known, that the portico with the barley-sugar columns is his. According to E. M. Beloe, a trustworthy local historian, the new front first stood athwart the street. Later the property was acquired by the Clifton family, and at that point the name of the house seems to have settled down for good.

This is the fourth consecutive note in which allusion has been made to Henry Bell. He lived from 1653 to 1717 and, like that other eminent provincial architect, John Carr, whom we shall meet in Yorkshire, he was twice mayor of the city he did so much to adorn. But that seems to be all; and it is presumably to this surprising scantiness of information that we must attribute the failure of the usual, as well as the more specialized, volumes of reference to pay him the acknowledgement that is surely his due or even to recognize his existence—an unfortunate contribution to the neglect of one of the earliest and most gifted of our provincial architects. Unlike Carr and the Woods, he never got the chance to show what he could do on a big scale, but within the limits allotted him he was invariably satisfying and delightful. Fortunately he has won influential friends, including both Mr. Christopher Hussey and Mr. Sacheverell Sitwell. But though the former, in his *Supplement to Blomefield's Norfolk*, put himself to great pains to trace his history and seemed, at one moment, to be establishing Roger Pratt as his teacher, he was forced in the end, for lack of evidence in any direction, to leave the problem little advanced.

Clifton House, King's Lynn.   Barbara Jones 1942

ALL SAINTS', MORSTON

Martin Hardie, C.B.E.

Remote, bleak, even desolate, the north coast of Norfolk between Hunstanton and Cromer has its peculiar charm. To the North Sea and the sand-dunes the little fishing-villages are joined by an occasional creek or causeway through wide marshes empty of anything, even of stunted trees, which might break the north-easterly gales. At one time the strip of waste land extended much deeper; you could see, so people said, two rabbits quarrelling over one blade of grass. But in the last quarter of the eighteenth century a great agriculturist, Coke of Norfolk, turned his estate at Holkham, a few miles to the west of Morston, into rich and profitable land, and now all the country south of the marsh has been taught to thrive. But the district is still, as it always has been, the home of sailors—sailors of all kinds, including Captain Marryat, who lived and died at Langham.

The subject of this drawing—a remarkably skilful record in which atmosphere is combined with strict fidelity—is typical of the coast roadside. The view is of the south or landward wall of the church, and the reader must imagine the marsh, behind the houses to right and left, stretching to the strips of yellow sand and grey sea a mile away.

All Saints', standing on a mound, is built of flint rubble, the usual material of houses hereabouts. In its churchyard there are even graves of flint, flat, coffin-shaped, supine in the grass. It is, in appearance, as simple, bluff, and sturdy as the fishermen who worship there—and as well worth knowing. It possesses an early rood-screen of eight painted panels; a font finely carved, in the shape of a Maltese Cross; and a mural tablet, beautiful and grim with skull, bell, hour-glass, and poem to the memory of Susan King, who died in 1615, aged 23.

YORKSHIRE

Artists

JOHN COOPER	IRENE HAWKINS	MICHAEL ROTHENSTEIN
JOHN GAULD	E. B. MUSMAN	KENNETH ROWNTREE, A.R.W.S.
MARTIN HARDIE, C.B.E.	HORACE ROOKE	EDWARD WALKER

BESIDES being unequal in size, the three great divisions of Yorkshire are rather misleading in name; for all the southern part of the county is included in the East or the West Riding, whilst half of the east coast and a good slice of the western boundary fall within the North Riding. The East Riding is the smallest of the three and the least industrialized. As for the most highly industrialized district, the West Riding, almost all considerations had to give way to the urgent recording of a tract of country which was, in 1940, about to disappear beneath Sheffield's vast new reservoir. Of houses, farms, and bridges along the Derwent valley which are now hidden by water, a number of drawings was secured; but though the Reservoir Extension Scheme is for the relief of Sheffield and its environs, the area submerged lies just over the border and the records belong to Derbyshire.

So it comes about that most of the county drawings in the collection and almost all those reproduced here are of the North Riding. It offers enough, and more; for, though smaller than the West Riding, it is larger than any English county except Lincolnshire and Devonshire. Beginning where all the Ridings begin, at York, it fans out to Westmorland and Durham; its eastern boundary is the North Sea, its western stretches to a point little more than twenty miles from the Irish Sea; and it is full of wild country, fine towns, and famous ruins.

Spaciousness seems to beget spaciousness, as Americans know. In Yorkshire the mansions, the abbeys, the landscape itself tend to be enormous. They also tend to have been recorded already, by Turner, by Cotman, and by hundreds of painters on holiday. Here will be found nothing of York Minster, of Wentworth or Castle Howard, or of the great Cistercian abbeys save one whose name (Byland) is better known to antiquarians than to the ordinary traveller. The artists were sent in search of smaller game as a rule and, true to intention, they returned with humbler buildings, views less renowned; scenes which, after long and unpretentious careers, have acquired the dignity always conferred by defencelessness.

THE OLD PRISON, YORK

John Cooper

The Old Prison at York, facing us in the drawing, was built in 1705, becoming the New Prison at York and the latest of a series of prisons going back, with ever darker and crueller histories, for 600 years. In all England few sites have so dreadful a record. The right wing was principally occupied by debtors, but the Governor and certain members of his staff were housed there, too. In the left wing the felons were confined; and all prisoners had, as their exercise ground, part of the courtyard in front. John Wesley inspected the new establishment and thought highly of it, but from details available to-day his opinion must be taken as an indictment of other prisons rather than a vindication of York.

The Assize Courts on the right of the picture were built by John Carr in 1777 and are still employed for their original purpose. (Opposite, across the square, is a similar block built in 1780 as administrative offices, but later converted into a Women's Gaol and now the Castle Museum.) A gallows was erected behind the Courts. Hitherto, men had been hanged on open ground outside the city, and the popularity of the spectacle had seriously incommoded trade and industry. The new site, affording restricted views, was expected to lessen the general enjoyment; but the forerunners of our football crowds proved, like their descendants, difficult to balk. As late as 1862 (according to a local historian) special excursion trains brought sightseers from the rural areas. Given a good programme the crowd would number 10,000 persons including many children, with thimble-riggers and vendors of fruit and nuts helping the holiday atmosphere.

At one time the courtyard (where the lawn became a vegetable garden in 1942) was much used for political meetings. During the revolt of the freeholders against the great county families, in the ninth decade of the eighteenth century, there was a tremendous day. It was in March 1784; the weather was appalling; and by the time the Fitzwilliam and Cavendish parties had finished their canvassing, the afternoon was far advanced. 'I saw', wrote Edward Gibbon, 'what seemed a mere shrimp mount upon the table; but as I listened, he grew, and grew, until the shrimp became a whale.' The shrimp was Wilberforce; and somehow, through the howling gale, he made his voice tell and carried the day for Pitt and against the Whig aristocracy so long in dominion. As his speech ended, a messenger from Pitt brought him news that the King had dissolved Parliament.

John Cooper

HOUSE IN CASTLEGATE, YORK

Irene Hawkins

Besides the Assize Courts of the previous picture, other and fairly numerous works by John Carr exist in and near York. Here, in Castlegate, we can study his Anglo-Palladian style employed in domestic architecture. The house was built not later than 1770 for Charles Gregory, 9th Viscount Fairfax. During the war the main structure became a canteen centre, while the farther portion, on the left, met a still more anxious fate and was turned into a cinema. Nevertheless, the frontage has not greatly changed since this drawing was done.

Already, in the first two pictures of the county, we have twice met Carr of York, and we shall meet him again. Some account of this eminent provincial architect may interest readers south of the Trent, to whom he is merely a name—and often not even that.

Unlike James Wyatt, the elder Wood of Bath, Thomas Ripley and other Yorkshire architects who came south, John Carr (1723–1807) stayed at home. He was born near Wakefield and, after spending some years as a working mason, moved to York before he was thirty. He soon made a reputation for himself, in Derbyshire, Lancashire, Cheshire, Nottinghamshire, and Lincolnshire as well as in Yorkshire, and may be said to have dominated a very large area. An abridged list of his works (they are fully set out in the Architectural Publication Society's *Dictionary*) will give an idea of the extent of his practice: the Grand Stand, York race-course; Harewood House, near Leeds (rated his best performance); Lytham Hall, near Preston; Thoresby Lodge, for the Duke of Kingston; the east front of Wentworth Castle, for the Earl of Strafford; Town Hall and Assembly Room at Newark; the Crescent at Buxton; the Mausoleum at Wentworth House, for Earl Fitzwilliam; and Basildon Park, near Pangbourne, his solitary southern adventure.

He was a shrewd, active man, alive to the civic virtues and responsibilities and not entirely dead to their profitable uses. He was twice Lord Mayor of York; and, after rebuilding at his own expense the church of his native village, he left £150,000— a highly respectable sum, even for an eighteenth-century architect.

Houses in Coney, near the Castle, York.

Ivon Hawkins

CLIFF BRIDGE TERRACE AND MUSEUM, SCARBOROUGH

Kenneth Rowntree, A.R.W.S.

The seventeenth century was a great time for spas, and brought prosperity to Llandrindod, Epsom, Bath, Harrogate, Dulwich, Tunbridge Wells, and other curative centres. When, therefore, in the year 1620 or thereabouts, an intelligent woman named Mrs. Farrow noticed that certain water in the neighbourhood had a property which imparted a russet colour to the pebbles, she did her fellow-citizens of Scarborough a good turn. 'Several persons of quality', we are told, 'came from a great distance to drink it, preferring the waters of this spaw before all the others they had formerly frequented, even the Italian, French or German.'

When, later, sea bathing came into favour, Scarborough was there again, offering beautiful sands. The southern cliff was the first to become fashionable, and was thus fortunate enough to be developed during the Regency, of which period its terraces still provide pleasant examples. Between 1820 and 1840 the work was carried across the ravine to the promontory on the north, and to this era belongs the scene here depicted. Growth has continued ever since; signs of it, with which the artist's integrity has forbidden him to tamper, may be discerned in the drawing.

The old terrace looks across, and takes its name from, the long, pedestrian bridge leading over the valley to South Cliff. The Museum, twelve months younger than the bridge, was built for the Philosophical Society in 1828, to the design of Richard Hey Sharp, of York. 'A rotunda of the Doric order with wings', it was much used, after its opening in 1830, for lectures. Compact and distinctive, it seems the very place for the purpose, or for the display of a choice collection; but, in fact, it is crammed with the customary, if harmonious, assembly of stuffed birds, fossils, and the white-washed busts of local worthies. Little visited and slightly forlorn it retains, for any occasional visitor who may glance in its direction, the good manners of its age.

As likely as not, it is the first of Sharp's works, for in the year of its construction he left Peter Atkinson, to whom he had been apprentice and, later, partner, and set up on his own. Atkinson had been John Carr's assistant and, at his death, his professional heir. The little Museum thus embodies much local architectural tradition.

30 SANDSIDE, SCARBOROUGH

Kenneth Rowntree, A.R.W.S.

Down by the harbour, at sea-level or clinging unsteadily, tier above tier, to the face of the cliff, are far older buildings—many of them, like the one shown here, falling into decay, or else being replaced by cafés and shops for the summer visitors. The best of the survivors are worth recording. This is the old town. From the top of the cliff or scar the ruins of the castle or burgh can be seen looking down on Scarborough.

As in harbour-sides all over the world, the area is at once split up and joined up by endless alleyways. At the corners of the narrow streets and courts, bearing some such revealing title as 'Mast Yard', little groups of men wearing raincoats over blue jerseys gather together, for company rather than conversation. The bars are frequent, friendly, and snug.

In 1283, when Edward I was king, Scarborough was one of the nineteen boroughs to be represented in Parliament. In time, Hull usurped its place as a port; but, as has already been mentioned, Scarborough found a second lease of life as a spa, and a third as a holiday resort.

Kennett Rowntree '40

NEWBURGH PRIORY

Michael Rothenstein

The site of the old house was selected by Roger de Mowbray, in 1145, for an Augustinian priory. When, under Henry VIII, so much religious property was destroyed or sold or given away, the estate was presented to one Belasyse, and he began the process of turning the ruined remains into a dwelling. The family continued to prosper, and one of his descendants was created Lord Fauconberg by Charles I.

The present house is uneven in shape and age. It contains, in addition to pieces of the old priory, traces of thirteenth-, fourteenth-, and fifteenth-century masonry, but the central block dates from about 1600, and the east wing is a further and subsequent addition. The corner shown here, half hidden by a clipped yew, is the north-west, and just to the right of the tree can be seen, in the middle of the west front, the archway leading to the stable-yard. The many remarkable examples of topiary, the trees and lakes of the surrounding park, the heavy iron gates at the end of the short drive, the beautiful colour of the limestone material used by the builders, and even the irregularity of the mansion combine to produce an effect of unusual charm, of mingled formality and informality.

The second Lord Fauconberg, though the bearer of a nearly new title bestowed by a lately executed sovereign, married Oliver Cromwell's daughter, Mary. Besides preserving her father's sword, saddle, and watch, she is said to have recovered his dishonoured body from the gibbet at Tyburn and to have buried it, walled up, in the house.

On the north, the property marches with the southern end of Byland, which we shall shortly be visiting. Indeed, the five or six pictures and notes beginning here with Newburgh form a little group full of reflections and cross-reflections; the same places and persons, names and dates, constantly recur. There is nothing peculiar to Yorkshire or even to Britain in this close-woven pattern of local history; all the more, perhaps, is it worth illustrating for that reason, when a good opportunity offers.

OLD TANNERY, COXWOLD

Michael Rothenstein

All round Coxwold lies the Laurence Sterne country. At Sutton-in-the-Forest, eight miles to the south, he was installed in 1738, and there wrote the first two parts of *Tristram Shandy*. In 1744 he was presented, in addition, with the living of Stilling-ton, two miles nearer to Coxwold. In 1760 his friend, Lord Fauconberg, made him (still in addition) perpetual curate of Coxwold; and there, when not rushing to London or travelling on the Continent, he remained till his death, in London, eight years later. During these years at Shandy Hall, on the edge of the village, he wrote, as always, feverishly, concluding *Tristram Shandy*, issuing a second series of *Sermons* 'abounding in unclerical humour', and producing *A Sentimental Journey*.

For years, almost all his life, he had been overtaxing his delicate constitution, living (as we should say) on his nerves; and the wonder is not that the comparative peace of Coxwold should have failed to restore him but that it did not induce a swift collapse. He seems to have been happy there—at least he said he was, 'as happy as a prince . . . 'tis a land of plenty. I sit down alone to venison, fish, and wild fowl, or a couple of fowls or ducks; with curds, strawberries and cream. . . . I have a hundred hens and chickens about my yard, and not a parishioner catches a hare or a rabbit, or a trout, but he brings it as an offering to me.' Material rather than spiritual consolation, no doubt; but, by the standards of 1946, pretty solid.

From a lowly beginning the village scrambles up a steep hill to where, at the top, stands the fine church. It is strikingly like the church at Thirsk, and in fact both rectorial tithes were held by the Prior of Newburgh; but the church where Sterne preached has far the finer monuments, especially those of the Protector's son-in-law (mentioned in the preceding note) and other members of the Belasyse or Faucon-berg family.

The old tannery, and the scarcely younger farm in which it now serves, will have been seen often enough by the restless clergyman in his walks abroad. They form, together, a modest corner of an unspoiled village, one of the most memorable in Yorkshire.

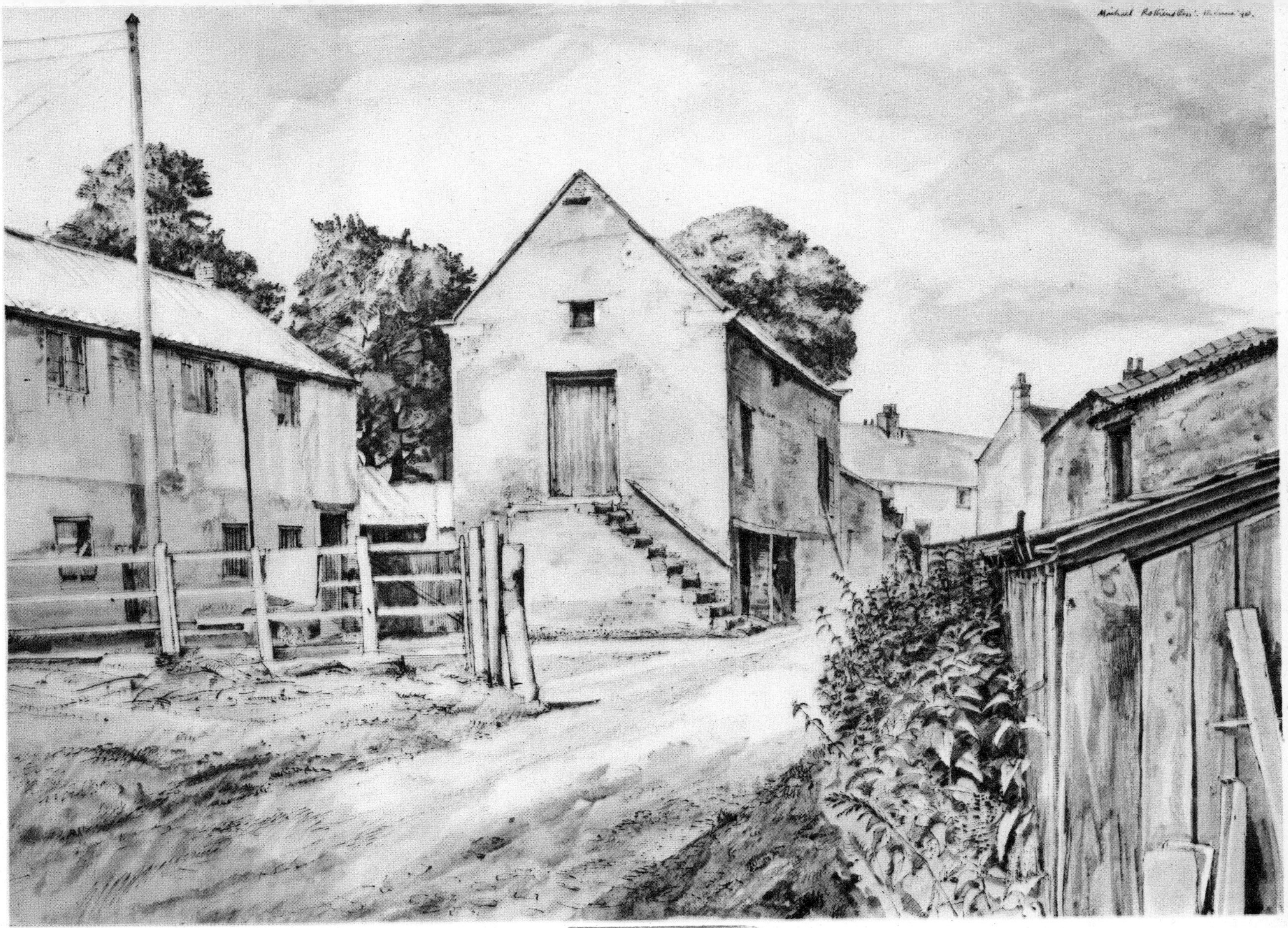

BYLAND ABBEY, FROM THE WEST

Michael Rothenstein

In beauty and in interest, the ruined Cistercian abbeys of Yorkshire are nowhere surpassed; and Byland, if less renowned and less picturesquely sited than Fountains and Rievaulx, ranks high among them. It stands two miles from Coxwold and four from Rievaulx to which, as will be seen, it promised at one time to be much nearer.

A charming account of the foundation of the house was left by Philip, third Abbot, 'as he heard it from his predecessor, Abbot Roger', but it is a leisurely affair, starting at the Fall of our first parents in the Garden of Eden, and must here be rudely compressed. In or about 1137 the Abbot of Calder and some of the brethren left Furness in Lancashire, inaugurated ten years before, and set out to found a new monastery. Their journey was interrupted by an invasion of the country by David, King of Scotland, and they returned to Furness. They were not well received and, with their worldly goods in a wagon drawn by eight oxen, they set out again, this time for York. At Thirsk the Lady Gundreda, mother of Roger de Mowbray, showed hospitality to the holy men and, to end their wanderings, settled them at Hode, under the eye of an uncle of hers who had turned hermit. In 1143 Roger de Mowbray moved them to a spot almost opposite to Rievaulx across the Rye. 'Abbot Roger and his monks remained upon the Rye five years. The intention and purpose of Roger de Mowbray had been that the abbey should, if possible, be built on the south bank of the river Rye, in order that we might receive in all respects the same advantages and easements from the water which the monks of Rievaulx enjoy on the north bank. But the situation of the place rendered this impossible; the two houses were too near each other to allow of it, for at every hour of the day and night the one convent could hear the bells of the other, and this was unseemly and could not in any way long be borne.'

So they moved again, to Stocking; and once more and finally in 1177 when, forty years after leaving Furness, they found a site that suited them and they built their abbey. The west front, mounting to the imposing rim of the Catherine-wheel window, is the most complete of the walls, but a fair amount of the north side is also standing; and the roof having gone and the light within being the same as the light without, pieces of the Hambleton Hills appear in the vacant window-shapes like details extracted for our closer observation.

LODGE, THIRKLEBY PARK

Irene Hawkins

The mansion of Thirkleby Park was built for the Frankland family in 1780–5, to the design of James Wyatt. Without even being replaced by an inferior affair, it was pulled down some years ago, and now nothing remains but the servants' quarters (or some of them) and this entrance lodge.

It stands a mile or so to the south-east of Thirsk, on the main Easingwold road. The big house has withdrawn its support; the drive, its purpose gone, has lost hope and self-respect; and the lodge seems to wait forlornly for an end that cannot be long delayed. But whether, as some believe, it should be credited to Carr of York or, as seems more likely, to Wyatt, it is a little masterpiece of elegance, of proportion, of deceptively easy-looking grace. The colour of the stone is of great beauty; and, on closer inspection, the care and finished skill revealed in the medallions and other ornaments add simultaneously to our pleasure and to our helpless forebodings.

Moel Hebog Cottage, by the Cwm of [...]

THE PAVILION ON THE TERRACE, DUNCOMBE PARK

Kenneth Rowntree, A.R.W.S.

Guide-books recommend the visitor to obtain his first sight of Rievaulx Abbey from the terrace of Duncombe Park. The celebrated, bird's-eye view has been recorded times without number; not so the old lawn with its classical buildings, whence the panorama is afforded.

The terrace was laid out in 1754, and an account of its amenities fifty years later occurs in Part XIV of the *Gentleman's Magazine*: 'The prodigious expense the predecessor of the present possessor was at to make a bowling-green on the brow of the hill that overlooks these ruins evinces that he had a superabundance of wealth but . . . knew the best way of doing good with it was to provide employment for the industrious. At one end of this green is an elegant pavilion and, at the other, a beautiful circular temple. . . . The gardener generally has a store of excellent ale for the refreshment of such as will be at the pains and labour of ascending the steep and intricate path which leads to this truly delightful spot from whence, on three sides, are most beautiful prospects; on the fourth, a thick planta-tion of firs and shrubs breaks the northern blasts. . . . Here Mr. Duncombe sometimes liberally entertains his friends, the pavilion being furnished with every conveniency for that purpose.'

What the writer, with the large ideas of his day, labels a bowling-green is, in fact, a curving sward some 40 yards across and half a mile in length. Here and there, too, other misleading phrases have crept into his note. But it is clear that the scene has not changed at all in 140 years. Within, the porticoed Ionic pavilion is still gay with Burnici's adorn-ments. Specially imported from Italy, he spent seven years, half of them on his back, covering walls and ceiling with copies of 'the most admired works of Guido, etc.'.

When Victoria's long reign had nearly completed its elevating mission, a current of those northern blasts seems to have penetrated the shrubbery and chilled the meridional, warm saloon. Among the first to wince at the juxtaposition of pagan images and the Cistercian abbey was Mr. Wheater, commentator in Jackson's *Illustrated Guide to York-shire* (1891). Detailing 'Apollo driving the chariot of the Sun, attended by the smiling Houris [*sic*] and Cupid holding a torch', he goes on to point out that 'the incongruity of these heathen scenes amid the ruins of a Christian temple gives rise to unpleasant thoughts. It is, however, a lesson of the vast degradation we suffered by restoring the house of Stuart and adopting the continental tastes they imported.'

Kenneth Rowntree '40

ASHBERRY BRIDGE

John Cooper

From Scawton Moor through Ashberry Woods to Ryedale the road to Helmsley drops 400 feet; and at the bottom, where the bridge crosses the river Rye, a turning to the north leads up a fold in the hills to Rievaulx Abbey, half a mile away, and Old Byland.

Between the years 1140 and 1200 the settled monks of Rievaulx and the unsettled monks who eventually built Byland pushed the bed of the Rye hither and thither. Even when they had finished, the site of Rievaulx was so restricted by water on one side and steep slope on the other that the abbey had to run almost north and south.

The bridge, consisting of three semicircular arches, is of no great antiquity— Jervoise dates it late eighteenth century—but it must have had many predecessors. It is particoloured, being grey (natural stone) on the south side and red-stained on the other. The edge of Scawton Moor can be seen in the background on the right.

ST. MARY THE VIRGIN'S, THIRSK

Michael Rothenstein

Locally the ancient town of Thirsk is known for its agricultural market, which serves, and has long served, a large area; to the tourist, armed with a guide-book, for its parish church, a fine embattled building in the Perpendicular style. It is yet another token of the indefatigable piety of Roger de Mowbray, whom we have met twice already. Thirsk was the family town where the family castle stood. With the King of Scotland, Roger rebelled against Henry II; but the revolt failed, and the castle was demolished. With Henry's rebellious son and heir, Richard Cœur de Lion, Roger was on far better terms, and he served under him with much distinction in the Holy Land. But he seems to have made no attempt to restore the castle, preferring to use the ruins to provide material for the church on the other side of the town. Assuming the truth of all this, we may place the date of St. Mary the Virgin's in the last quarter of the twelfth century.

Although restored more than once, the building is of unusual purity of style. With its Lion of Mowbray, its relics from Byland Abbey, its transference, early in its career, to the Priors of Newburgh, and its windows painted by the loving hands of the ladies of Thirkleby Park, it illustrates once again, and very forcibly, the close texture of the local history.

SUNNY TERRACE, NORBY

Michael Rothenstein

Norby is the name of the northern extremity of Thirsk, where the road, after passing the church, partners the river Caldbeck and disappears with it across country to Thornton le Street.

The drawing shows the stream in the foreground, Sunny Terrace beyond, the road that divides them, with the open country for which it is making on the right. The interest of the picture lies in the age and position of the old cottages. They are the last houses in Thirsk, and they seem to indicate that this busy town has not made any extension northward for a surprisingly long while. The explanation immediately suggesting itself—that Norby was a separate village only recently reached by the town—is unacceptable, for one looks in vain for new buildings at the southern end of Norby or the northern end of Thirsk proper.

MIDDLEHAM CASTLE

Martin Hardie, C.B.E.

Descriptions of this famous castle, available in any guide book, make rather dull reading unless supported by a visit. Historical details, if a little less easily accessible, are more dramatic when found.

The castle was built in 1191 by a great-nephew of Alan of Brittany who (as will appear in a page or two) founded the castle at Richmond. In the following century it passed by marriage to the Nevilles and became one of their principal northern strongholds; and it was still in their possession when, two centuries later, its lord was Richard Neville, Earl of Warwick, nick-named the Kingmaker. In the turbulent days of the Wars of the Roses he played so great a part that he genuinely earned this imposing by-name. He dethroned Henry VI, proclaimed Edward IV as king, quarrelled with him and drove him from the country, and replaced Henry on the throne. That was as far as he got, for Edward, returning at the head of an army, defeated and slew the Earl at the Battle of Barnet in 1471. Both Henry VI and (according to Holinshed) Edward IV were, at different times, Warwick's prisoners at Middleham. The new owner of the castle was his son-in-law, the Duke of Gloucester, who twelve years later became ruler of the country under the name of Richard III. His son—the Kingmaker's grandson—was born at Middleham in 1473 and died there in 1484. Richard was devoted to the place and, in view of the odious reputation lastingly bestowed on him by Tudor historians, it is worth noting that Middleham was devoted to him. Bacon, in his *History of Henry VII*, found himself forced to make frequent, and embarrassed, allusions to Richard's popularity in Richmondshire—e.g. 'the old humour of these countries where the memory of King Richard was so strong . . . that it lay, like lees, in the bottom of men's hearts, and if the vessel was but stirred it would come up'.

The massive old fortress—it has walls 10–12 feet thick—is not remarkable for beauty; but, as has been shown, it played its part in our history, and it has a place in our literature, too. The Decorated castle was built round the Norman keep by the Neville who, as 1st Earl of Westmorland, is familiar to us in Shakespeare's *Henry IV*. Many of the scenes in Bulwer Lytton's *Last of the Barons* are laid in Middleham.

MIDDLEHAM—NEAR THE CASTLE

E. B. Musman

Here is another view of Middleham, showing that the castle is not, from all angles, the disengaged block of the previous drawing. And there the picture might be left, if it were not that the little houses suggest the little men who, in fact, make up a fair proportion of the local population.

For on the moor outside the town horses have been galloped and 'lads' of all ages have ridden them since the seventeenth century. It was from these training-grounds of Middleham that, in 1945, the great Dante went down to win the Derby, thus stemming a very long succession of southern triumphs—seventy-five, no northern-trained horse having won the race since Pretender, in 1869. He, too, came from the Middleham gallops.

The excitement of finding himself among the famous horses and horsemen of the North Riding proved almost too much for Defoe. His rapture mounts from sentence to sentence until, in the tone of a man who, after good entertainment, has been chatted unawares into the purchase of a nice hack, he bids the world ransack its stables to find a horse to equal the Yorkshire-bred.

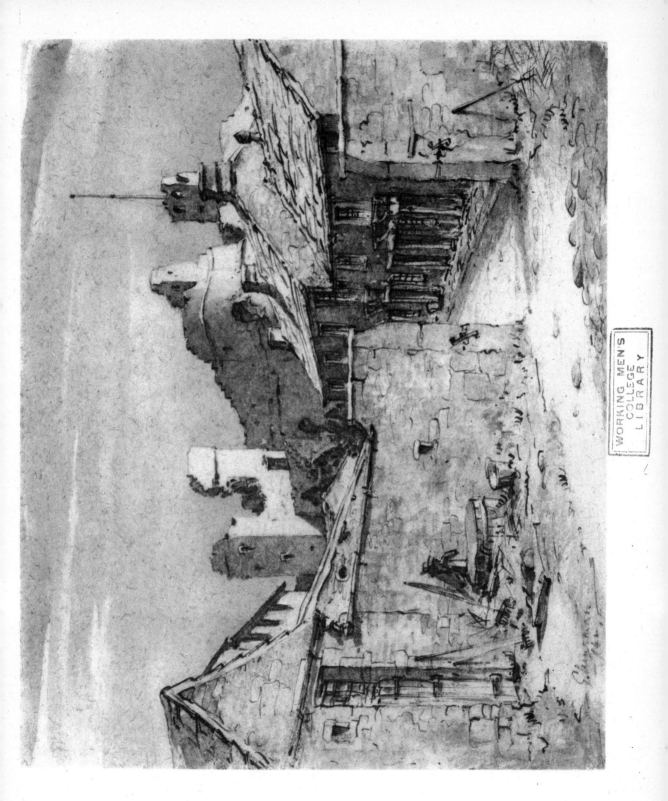

REETH

E. B. Musman

A large village in a magnificent setting eleven miles west of Richmond, Reeth is the eastern entrance to a stern, wild tract of country beloved of bold pedestrians—Arkengathdale and Upper Swaledale. Reeth itself is 600 feet above sea-level, yet it lies in a saucer whose steep sides rise in a three-quarter circle of surrounding heights mounting, at one point, to more than 2,000 feet.

The view given here is of the opening on the Richmond side, of the valley through which the road runs beside the Swale. During the years of the war there has been much felling of timber on the precipitous banks, but the river, gurgling and splashing along its deep channel, is still sufficiently romantic. The rivers that meandered through Volume I—the placid Ouse, the gentle Lea, the smooth Thames—bear little resemblance to the broken, swashing courses of the north and west.

> The savage spirit of old Swale is roused,
> He howls amid his foam

—so wrote William Mason, remembered as the friend and literary executor of Gray if now forgotten as a poet. He was making no great demands on poetic licence. These northern streams, so pretty and playful in summer, are liable in winter to sudden and most destructive violence. When, as he made his famous Tour, he reached this part of the island, the creator of the dauntless Crusoe and Moll Flanders could not conceal his alarm. At that time, in the 1720s, the roads of England were little removed from their most abject state; a flooding river was a disaster and a danger; and Defoe, like a traveller in Tibet or Lapland, was at great pains to draw for his readers a picture of these far, incredible torrents.

Metaphorically as well as literally, he couldn't get over them. Already in Nottinghamshire his apprehensions had been aroused by the Trent, 'a most outrageous stream'. In Derbyshire the Derwent is 'that Fury of a River . . . we kept our Distance, the Waters being out; for the *Derwent* is a frightful Creature when the Hills load her Current with Water; I say, we kept our Distance'. The Tees he described as 'a most terrible River'. He cannot have been aware of what the Swale can achieve when in earnest, or so nervous a traveller would never have contented himself with 'a noted River . . . has some unevenness at its Bottom, by reason of Rocks which intercept its Passage, so that it falls like a Cataract, but not with so great a Noise'.

CASTLE TERRACE, RICHMOND

E. B. Musman

Richmond, even without the great castle in the midst of it, would seem a fortress. It stands on a precipitous rock, round the base of which the broken Swale 'makes sweet music with the enamell'd stones'; and the town itself, as well as its approaches, is often crazily steep. From this drawing of a typically rugged corner the road behind us drops sharply; the central square itself slants at an alarming angle, so that at the top end one looks, through alleyways or even through houses, if both back and front doors happen to be open, out into space. This square is full of character. Elsewhere there are noble ruins and relics, but here the old buildings still fulfil their function. Besides a church, partly let out in shops and dwellings, and a hotel with a magnificent façade, good shop-fronts and inns line the cobbled road on all sides.

When the resisting Earl Eadwine died in 1072, the Conqueror granted his demesne to Alan the Red, a son of the Duke of Brittany. With 164 local manors in his pocket, he made Richmond his headquarters and founded the immense castle of which the main tower, as can be seen, is still a most solid piece of masonry. He became the 1st Earl of Richmond. A subsequent holder of the title was Henry VII, and when he built a palace near Sheen, in Surrey, he gave it the name of Richmond. The 1st Duke of Richmond was Henry Fitzroy, a natural son of Henry VIII; but the titles constantly lapsed and were renewed until, in 1675, Charles Lennox became the 1st Duke of the existing line.

He was three years old, and one of the natural sons of Charles II. His mother— baby-faced, scheming, avaricious, courageous, loathed—was Louise de Kéroualle, from Brittany; and the old, and frequently renewed, link between Richmond and Brittany now took on fresh complications. At Charles II's instigation, Louis XIV granted her the fief of Aubigny, in Brittany, which had reverted to the French crown on the death of Charles Stewart, an earlier Duke of Richmond, on whose family it had been bestowed, in 1422, by Charles VII of France.

There was a time when, for a long way round, the area was known as Richmond-shire, and the old name still lingers. Defoe, writing in 1725, refers to a rival claim set up by a gentleman who called himself Sir Solomon Swale, of Swale Hall, in Swale Dale, in the County of Swale. His family name was not, in his opinion, taken from the river but given to it.

ST. MARY'S, WHITBY—EXTERIOR

Kenneth Rowntree, A.R.W.S.

The parish church of Whitby occupies an exposed, magnificent site beside the ruined abbey on the eastern cliff-top. From the middle of its large churchyard it looks down on the harbour; and it must be conspicuous to sailors many miles from shore.

St. Peter's church, built in 657, probably stood on this spot. Two hundred years later it was destroyed by the Danes, and a quarter of a century seems to have passed without any attempt at reconstruction. Then, very early in the twelfth century, what may be called the present church arose. Certain of the Norman features still exist; but the building has undergone so many modifications during the intervening centuries, especially the thirteenth, fourteenth, seventeenth, eighteenth, and nineteenth, that even informed writers differ widely in their deductions and ascriptions. One of the most unusual of the eighteenth-century features is visible in the drawing, an outside staircase leading to the gallery. The gallery, as will be seen in the next picture, runs right round the church, and there are five of these stairways giving direct admission from the churchyard.

The approach to this wonderfully romantic building could—at least on paper—hardly be bettered, for it consists of 199 curving, shallow, stone steps. A good description occurs in Mrs. Gaskell's novel, *Sylvia's Lovers*, where Whitby figures under the name of Monkshaven. The book was published in 1863; though its story deals with the French wars sixty or seventy years earlier, a modern reader finds it hard to determine what reliance can be placed on the author's powers of reconstruction. For our purpose, it hardly matters.

'You could see the church stair, as it was called, from nearly every part of the town, and the figures of the numerous climbers, diminished by distance, looked like a busy ant-hill, long before the bell began to ring.... It was a good situation for that church. Home-ward-bound sailors caught sight of the tower, the first land object of all.... There, too, lay the dead of many generations, the large churchyard was rich in the dead. Masters, mariners, ship-owners, seamen; it seemed strange how few other trades were represented in that great plain so full of upright gravestones. Here and there was a memorial stone, placed by some survivor of a large family, most of whom perished at sea:—"Supposed to have perished in the Greenland seas", "Shipwrecked in the Baltic", "Drowned off the coast of Iceland". There was a strange sensation, as if the cold sea-winds must bring with them the dim phantoms of these lost sailors, who had died far from their homes, and from the hallowed ground where their fathers lay.'

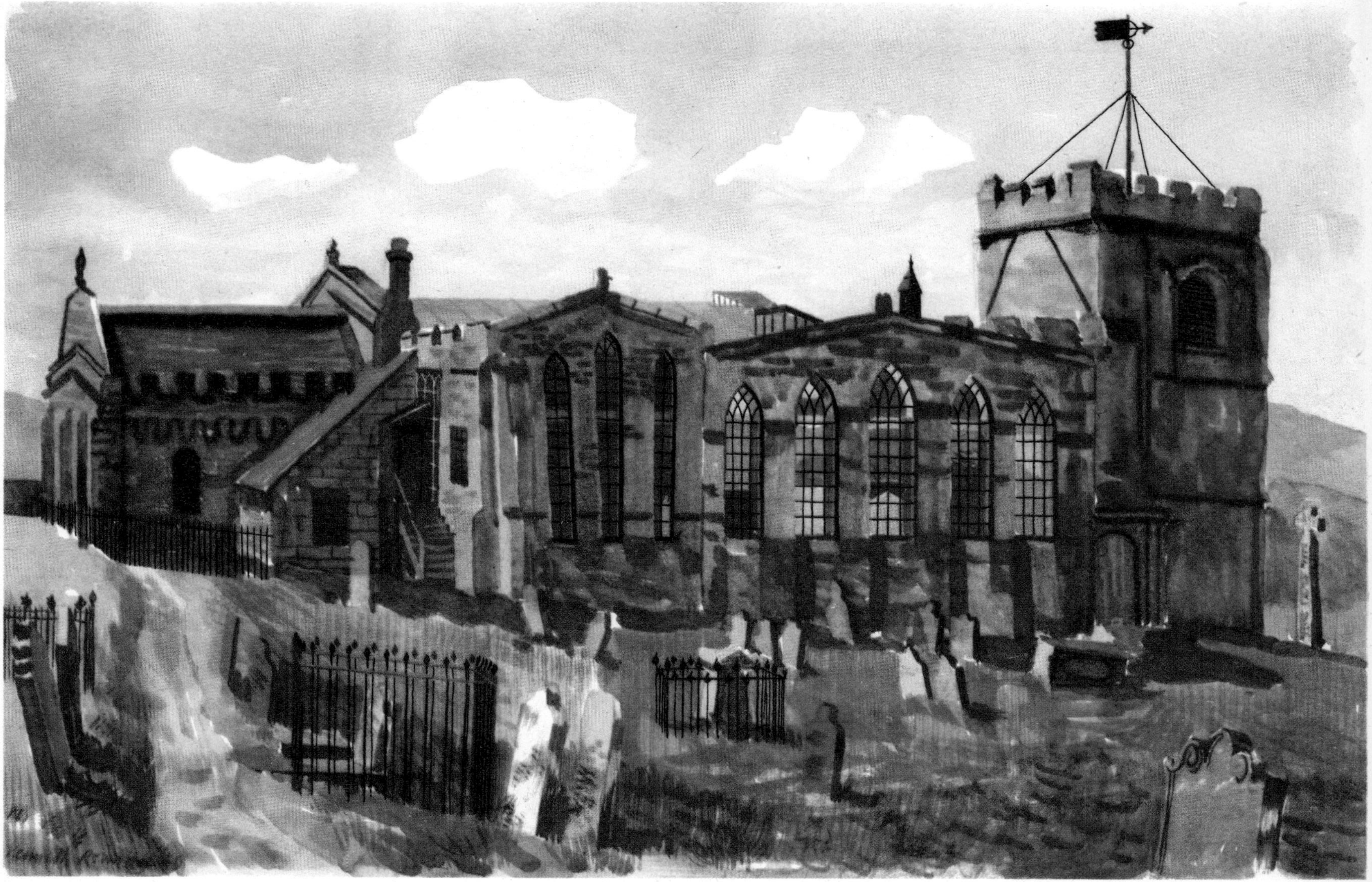

ST. MARY'S, WHITBY—INTERIOR

Horace Rooke

'The church', wrote Mrs. Gaskell, 'was . . . low and massive outside; inside, of vast space, only a quarter of which was filled on ordinary Sundays. The walls were disfigured by numerous tablets of black and white marble intermixed, and the usual ornamentation of that style of memorial as erected in the last century, of weeping willows, urns, and drooping figures, with here and there a ship in full sail, or an anchor, where the seafaring idea prevalent through the place had launched out into a little originality. There was no wood-work, the church had been stripped of that, most probably when the neighbouring monastery had been destroyed. There were large square pews, lined with green baize, with the names of the families of the most flourishing ship-owners painted white on the doors; there were pews, not so large, and not lined at all, for the farmers and shopkeepers of the parish.'

Except that we are apt to-day to admire the tablets of the eighteenth and early nineteenth centuries, her description remains true enough, as far as it goes. The high pews lined with baize, puce or green, are still all there with the names painted on the doors, and the unlined pews, too. But much that she did not think worth mentioning leaps to the eye to-day; and since the author of *Cranford* did not lack powers of observation, we are forced to conclude, even after allowing for changes of taste, that many features of the old church which delight us now were, in 1863, before the full fury of the Victorian restorers had been wreaked, too ordinary to call for comment. For obvious example, there is the great three-decker pulpit. The doors of the pews immediately beneath it—some of the pews date from James I—are labelled 'For Strangers Only'. Why were the best seats reserved for strangers? Was hospitality the motive? Or the vicar's wish to have them under his eye? Or the reluctance of the regular congregation to occupy pews where drowsiness was bound to be detected?

The gallery's fourth side (known locally as the Cholmley Pew) built, about 1700, across the chancel arch is something very seldom seen nowadays. The roof, or ceiling, is said to be the work, in 1612, of ships' carpenters, and indeed it much resembles it; and under the roof are cabin-like windows also, probably of the eighteenth century. In the transepts the pews are raked like seats in a theatre; and from the back rows one can look, through the clear and draughty window behind one's head, far out over what Mrs. Gaskell always called the German Ocean.

HAGGERSGATE, WHITBY

John Cooper

Running back up the mouth of the Esk, Whitby's long harbour, close-set with houses, is divided into two by a swinging bridge; and to this point converge the four chief streets mentioned in the charter granted to the town by the Abbot Richard in the twelfth century—Church Street on the right bank and Haggersgate, Flowergate, and Baxtergate on the left.

They still meet except for Haggersgate, whose southern end is now sealed off from the others by a block of buildings. But though shortened it has, in itself, suffered the least change, and the house on the right of the drawing is reputed to be the oldest in the port—a considerable claim in Whitby.

The houses in the background, where the road widens, stand on Fish Quay lining the seaward end of the harbour. All along this coast, once notorious for smuggling and always famous for fish, the fishermen use a peculiar boat called a coble—very pointed, nearly flat-bottomed, and usually too small for more than three men.

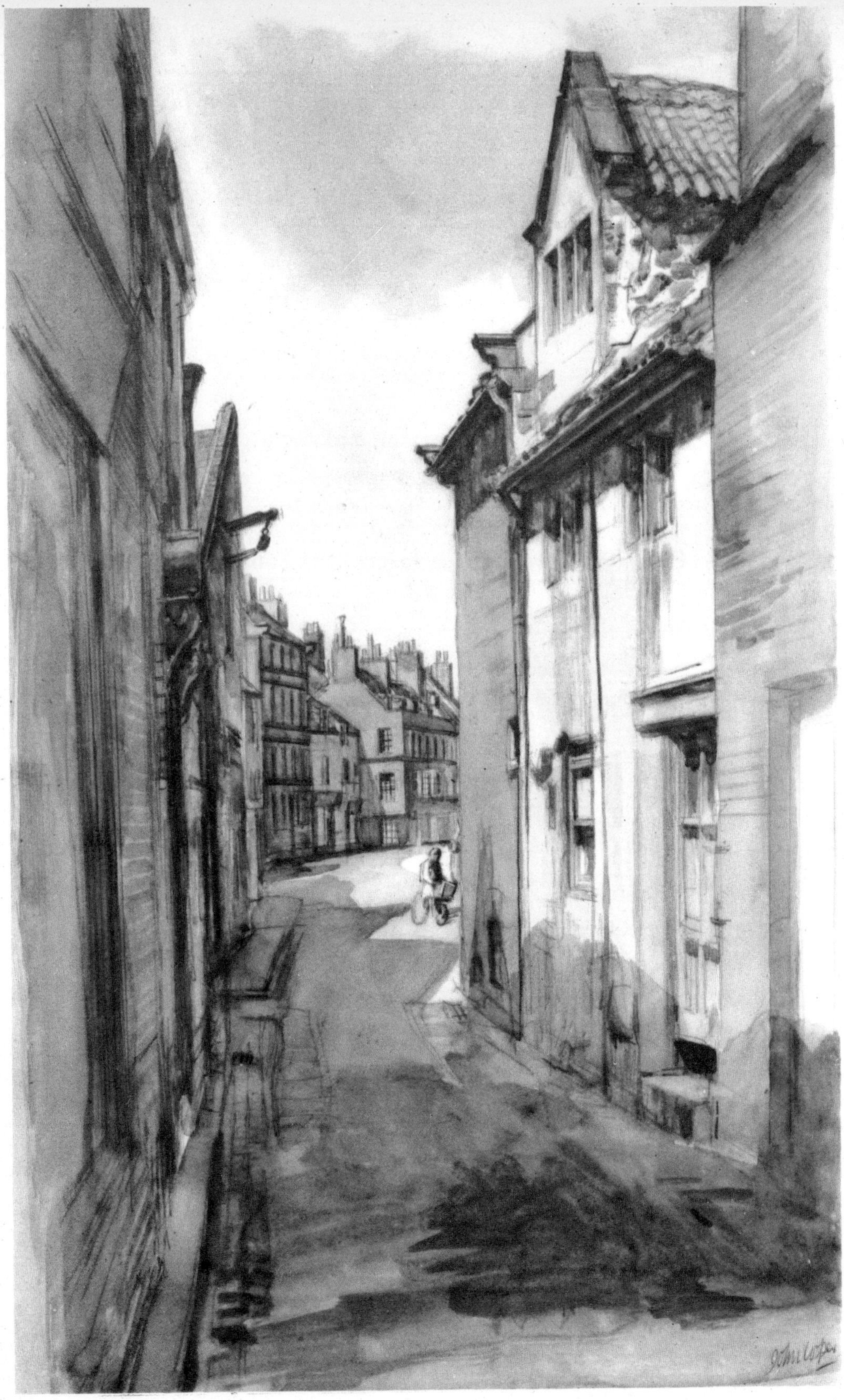

SANDSEND

John Cooper

Whitby is flanked on both sides by bays and creeks dear to the heart of the summer visitor—a little too dear for their perfect beauty. The cliff-tops have broken out into a rash of villas more likely to spread than to abate.

Robin Hood's Bay to the south-east (the famous outlaw is said to have kept fishing-vessels always ready here, in case the pursuit grew too hot) and the fishing-village of Staithes, to the north-west, have attracted so many artists that they are in no need of recording. But between Whitby and Staithes lie two little resorts whose appearance to-day may give future generations a few moments of incredulous amusement or anguish. The first of these is Sandsend, some three miles along the shore from Whitby. It has already a front, almost an esplanade; and an iron bridge overhead carries the railway lines across the ravine. But it is still a pretty little place with firm sands in front and pleasant woods behind, as well as the remains of a large alum quarry dating from the reign of James I.

RUNSWICK BAY

John Cooper

Four miles farther north comes the ampler, lovelier bay of Runswick. The extremities are so steep that the houses at the western end look down one another's chimneys, breathe down one another's necks; the paths, zigzagging amid the sandstone cottages, are bordered by front doors on one side and chimney-tops on the other; but between the two horns of the bay the ground runs back in a gentler slope covered with gorse, brambles, bracken, and elders—at any time of year a beautiful sight, threatened but not yet spoiled by 'permanent' bathing huts.

The stretch of coast was much favoured by fairies or bogles, the most amiable being Hob Thrush, who lived in a cavern, Hob Hole. He is reputed to have had so extensive a practice as a curer of the whooping-cough that, in his day, Runswick enjoyed a season all the year round. In addition, the cliffs are one of the chief sources of the famous Whitby jet—or were, until the industry drooped beneath the rising costs of the digging.

The trains run a mile or so inland; but the spreading settlement on the heights above the bay shows how man, with the aid of a good bus-service, can remedy the limitations of the railway track.

GRETA BRIDGE

Kenneth Rowntree, A.R.W.S.

For those who care to entertain them, the spot is rich in memories and emotions. Here Cotman, moving up and down, painted some of the most famous and beautiful of English water-colours; and a few hundred yards behind us, where the Greta, flowing northwards to the Durham border, makes its celebrated junction with the Tees, Turner stayed to render the scene. Between, along the bank of the river, Scott walked with his friend Morritt, the owner of the adjoining estate known as Rokeby; and in 1813, just before the bard merged into the novelist, he bestowed the name on one of the last of his long poems.

> The eve, that slow on upland fades,
> Has darker closed on Rokeby's glades,
> Where, sunk within their banks profound,
> Her guardian streams to meeting wound.
> The stately oaks, whose sombre frown
> Of noontide made a twilight brown,
> Impervious now to fainter light,
> Of twilight make an early night.
> Hoarse into middle air arose
> The vespers of the roosting crows,
> And with congenial murmurs seem
> To wake the Genii of the stream;
> For louder clamoured Greta's tide,
> And Tees in deeper voice replied.

The scene is hardly changed. The old coaching inn, on the left of the bridge, is as Cotman drew it. A stone column beneath a yew tree must have been seen, must surely have been sited, by Scott. Only the bridge itself is, for the time being, altered. Morritt had it built in 1789 to replace an older structure; and he did not foresee tanks and fuselages. So the balustrade has been removed and stored, and the roadway led over a Bailey-like bridge of pipes and tubes in front of the stone one. But soon after, or perhaps even before, these lines appear in print the balustrade will be replaced and the new bridge removed; and then, no doubt, Mr. Rowntree will cease to be the last of a long succession of artists to make his way to the banks of the Greta.

PRINTED IN GREAT BRITAIN
AT THE UNIVERSITY PRESS, OXFORD
BY CHARLES BATEY
PRINTER TO THE UNIVERSITY

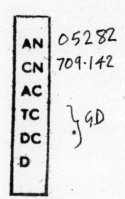